God Consciousness: Living with Meaning and Purpose

Robert M. Haralick

This book was prepared with LaTeX and set in 12 pt. by Robert M. Haralick.

10 9 8 7 6 5 4 ③ 2 1

The Tree of Life on the cover was designed by Sarah Bracha using a computer program that she wrote to generate the fractal tree.

Published by Torah Books 27 Tara Drive Pomona NY 10970
Printed by CreateSpace

ISBN 0-9722273-4-2

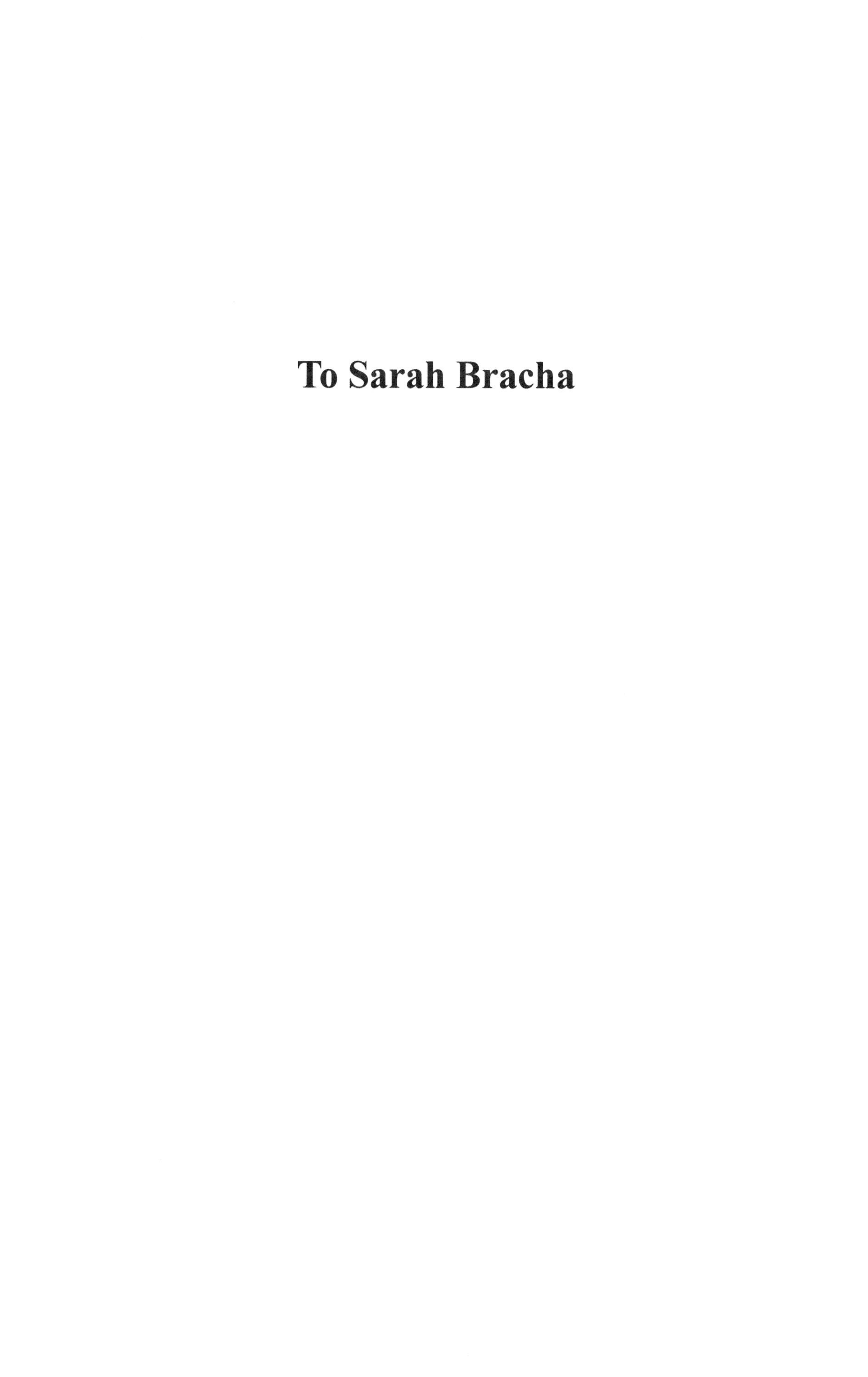

To Sarah Bracha

Contents

Working The Sefirot: Vices and Virtues

Living With Purpose

People who consciously live with meaning and purpose have an individual value and belief system[1] that guides their interpretations of everyday situations, guides their thoughts, their emotions, and their actions in a way that transcends the ordinary.

There are a variety of signposts that are associated with living purposefully. They include spending productive time on activities that matter the most and living through those activities with authenticity and passion. People living purposefully feel content and have an inner peace. The way they live not only makes a difference for themselves, but it makes a meaningful difference for the others in their circle. They live in the moment, in the eternal present. They are ethical and they meet all their commitments. They live life with intention. They live honestly, decently, joyfully, and authentically. They carry out what they hold to be their calling in life. They find meaning, purpose and significance in the ordinary everyday activities: eating, reading, working, and loving.

From a spiritual point of view, we are each a child of God. Our calling in some way shape or form is to manifest the glory of God that is uniquely within us in a useful and worthwhile way with balanced excellence. It means having a higher state of consciousness, a consciousness in which attention and intent is refined and a greater awareness of reality is present. It means being morally enlightened, serving a purpose greater than ourselves alone. It means passionate living in the manyfoldness of the world and yet perceiving and living in its unity and oneness. It means living life as sacred and holy.

Of course religion has a role in guiding people to recognize that there is something beyond themselves, guiding people to ethical and moral behavior. But when religion gets institutionalized with fixed ceremonies, or prayers, that are performed by rote, by force of habit, without feeling, without passion, automatically without conscious intent or choice once the ritual begins, spontaneity and consciousness of the eternal presence tends to be lost.

---

[1]Not all individual value and belief systems are equal. For example, consider someone whose value system is that the most important thing is to make it to the top, or a value system in which the most important thing is to ostentatiously have more than your neighbors. How about a value system in which the most important thing is to be a success, the goal, and any way to get there is OK, or a value system that without constraint maximizes their self interest. Such people will lie, take advantage of others, cheat and be ruthless, in general be corrupt, but they may make it to a roaring material success. Once there, some never get past that stage. Others find that eventually this is empty and without meaning. Other examples of shallow goals include having power, status and money. For people with these goals, whatever they have it is not enough. Since the goal is everything, their path to the goal can be unethical and unmoral.

When the external form becomes dominant. the main shell of what remains is the group social part, identification with the group and participation in the group. When the group shell becomes primary, the group is considered better than other groups. Self righteousness, elitism, prejudice and bigotism result. The same kind of thing happens in politics and it has disastrous consequences.[2]

Consciously living with meaning and purpose intensifies the living experience in ordinary everyday life, including in religious ceremonies. It is not only living in the present. It is living that transcends the present by becoming who we really are being. In the religious context, it provides a more intense form of religious experience than is generally found in normative religion. We experience peace, harmony and depth.

Our issue is what do we have to do to live with meaning and purpose in a spiritually authentic way. The approach we take involves understanding and practicing God Consciousness. First we deepen our understanding of consciousness and emotion so that we may be open to be more God conscious. Second we learn what kinds of behaviors promote God consciousness and what kind of behaviors lessen God consciousness.

In this volume, *God Consciousness: Living with Meaning and Purpose*, we do this from the discipline of Kabbalah: the teachings of giving and receiving; the teachings of unification; and the teachings of the Tree of Life. The teachings on giving and receiving and on unification set up context by which we can use the pattern of vices and virtues on a new form of the Tree of Life for understanding and transformation. Our outline is simple: on the one hand we must increase our individual knowledge and consciousness of God. On the other hand this increase happens with complete giving and receiving which is a kind of unification.

In the second volume of this work, *God Consciousness, Working the Sefirot and Netivot*, and we work with the theme that God consciousness cannot increase when our actions are actions of vice. But God consciousness can increase when our actions are actions of virtue. We repeat the basic teachings of the Tree of Life given in the first volume. Then we use the Tree of Life as an organizing

[2]For example, simply think of what can happen in nationalistic and/or imperialistic movements. Those who are considered inferior are trampled on, even killed. Think of the National Socialist German Worker party, the Nazis. What did Germany do to the other countries in Europe? What happened to the Jews? Think about what the Japanese did to the Chinese in starting in 1937, the rape of Nanjing, through to the surrender of Japan. Think about the religious wars: the European wars of religion of the 16th and 17th centuries, the Muslim conquest wars, the Crusades, the Spanish conquests, the Ottoman wars in Europe, the current wars of Islam against Christianity in Africa, ISIS against all others in the Middle East. All this happens when one group attempts to force their ways and goals on other groups. None of this kind of thing is spiritually authentic and in the end its only meaning or purpose for those experiencing the aggression is to survive.

principle for understanding vices and virtues. There, the main part of our work is the excercises: the prayer rituals using the vices and virtues on the tree of life to give us a moral context of what we want to become. They move us to a greater God consciousness. The exercises are not just exercises and they are not just rituals and they are not just prayers. In some sense they are beyond each of these. When done from the heart with care and from the soul with intent, they help transform us to be what we want to be.

Our context is the Kabbalah, the mystical teachings in Judaism. The religious texts we quote include the Torah and other Jewish texts, although not exclusively. Nevertheless because our approach is centered on authentic spirituality, it is ecumenical and holistic: our teaching of God consciousness is consistent with many religious traditions. Complete giving and receiving as well as working the Sefirot and Netivot, paths, on the Tree of Life is an individual practice that is compatible with all western and eastern religious and humanitarian traditions that emphasize ethics, morality and being a good person.

This first volume of God Consciousness gives over through essay, story, and poetry the intellectual, emotional, and spiritual perspective for understanding how to increase our God Consciousness. Each section must be slowly read, absorbed by the heart and integrated into our consciousness to have a full effect. There are a variety of sections which could have been formated as little essays. But they are formated poetically. This format gives space so you are not rushed to blindly read without absorbing what the section is inviting you to absorb. It would not be unusual to find yourself rereading a section multiple times to enjoy it and absorb its essence. It ends with the top level exercises on the Tree of Life. When done with full heart and intention, the exercises will work on the level of consciousness, subconsciousness, emotion, and soul and help move us to a greater God consciousness.

God Consciousness

There are two worlds, the world of God consciousness and the world without God consciousness. These two worlds on the outside appear the same, but on the inside are as different as different worlds can be. Indeed even on the outside they operate differently, but in a concealed way, not observable to a person without God consciousness. This is the meaning of

It is the honor of God to conceal a matter;[1]

To those without God consciousness, the world of God consciousness is concealed – not observable, not knowable, and not understandable.

The world of God consciousness, is a world of holiness, a world of completeness, perfection, and peace. It is a world of loving kindness, inner delight, joyfulness and thankfulness, an amazing world of the simplest and yet most intricate dancing and singing – truly a magical world. It is a world in which time, from moment to moment, is eternal.

The world of God consciousness is a miraculous world where nothing happens by chance. It is a world where everything that happens, is understood to happen by the hand of God, either directly or through the agency of another person or group of people. It is a world of a hiding and seeking dialog. The moment we lose God consciousness, God calls out: "See me! Do you see me?" God calls out to us to return to Him, to return to God consciousness. And we reply by our thoughts, speech, and action in a way that makes God's will our own will.

In the world of God consciousness, both that which is commonly taken to be good and that which is commonly taken to be bad for a person are all understood to happen by the hand of God. So in that deeper sense it is all good, for all that comes from God is absolutely good, even though sometimes we may not fully understand how that is so.

The world of God consciousness is a dynamic world of change. The very same thought, speech, or action that yesterday served to keep a person in the world of God consciousness may no longer do so today. The reason is that today God may have changed something in our situation to help us manifest a deeper virtue today than we could do yesterday. So today is actually a greater challenge than yesterday.

To stay in the world of God consciousness requires constant work and attention. The work is work to improve ourselves, to climb the next rung on our spiritual ladder, a ladder that brings us a situation requiring greater sensitivity, greater Godliness. And when we succeed, we move ourselves a littler closer to

[1]Proverbs .2:25

God. The attention is to keep our awareness focused so that when we slip out of the world of God consciousness, we are aware that this is what happened. In that way we can consciously move ourselves back into the world of God consciousness.

The world of God consciousness is a dynamic world of process: of bringing Godliness into our world so that our world becomes a place suitable to eternally dwell in God.

One of the traditions that teaches us how to live in the world of God consciousness is called the Torah. The Torah has a written and oral tradition. The written Torah includes the five books of Moses: Genesis, Exodus, Leviticus, Numbers, and Deuteronomy. These were given by God to the Israelites on Mount Sinai over thirty three hundred years ago. The rest of the written tradition includes books in the Writings, and the Prophets. The oral tradition encompasses the Mishnah, the Gemarah, the Aggadah, the Midrashim and the Kabbalah.

This book is a selection of Torah true teachings from the tradition explaining and illustrating some of the concepts we are required to know and live by in order that we can increase the opportunity of returning ourselves to, maintaining ourselves in, and transporting ourselves closer to the world of God consciousness. In this way the book is all about the second half of the verse in Proverbs first quoted.

> *It is the honor of God to conceal a matter; but it is the honor of kings to search out a matter.*

The world of God consciousness is a world of regalness, a world of royalty. For when we are able to live in a way that we experience the presence of God, God who is the King of Kings, we become in our own limited ways like Him, truly fulfilling the verse,

> *Let us make Man in Our image, after Our likeness. They shall rule over the fish of the sea, the birds of the sky, and over the animal, the whole earth, and every creeping thing that creeps upon the earth. So God created Man in His image, in the image of God He created him: male and female He created them.*[2]

There is a secret in those verses. The secret is not in the common meaning which is that mankind will dominate the earth and all the creatures on the earth. The secret is that the sea, the sky, and the earth referred to are all in each of us. The meaning of ruling or dominating is not that of ruling or dominating

[2]Genesis .1:26-27

over another. It is a ruling and dominating over that part of our own nature that is parallel to the fish of the sea, the birds of the sky, the animals and all the creeping things of the earth. It is this ruling over that we must do in order to move into and maintain ourselves in the world of God consciousness. And that is why we are Kings. The instruction book tells us that *it is the honor of kings to search out the matter*. With the help of God, that is what we shall do!

Consciousness

Consciousness is a word that can be used in many ways, often vaguely and ambiguously. Consciousness can mean sentience: the capability of sensing and responding to the world. It can mean sapience: the ability to perceive the relationship between oneself and one's environment. It can mean wakefulness. It can mean awareness or awareness of self. But none of these meanings is the meaning we intend.

Perhaps consciousness is most confused with awareness. Awareness is passive. We are aware. Its screen is the mind. We can see the room around us. We can be aware that another person is in the room. We can be aware of how we are standing or sitting. But each of these kinds of awareness is not consciousness. Awareness cannot make us more sensitive, more compassionate, or more loving. Awareness does not transform our limitations or lift us out of our limitations, but being more conscious can be transformative and lift us through our limitations.

Consciousness is active, even pro-active. Not only is there a passive awareness, but there is an active component of relating to what we are aware, of understanding the essence of what we are aware, and of being and acting the essence of who we are. In this sense, consciousness is more than an inner awareness or self reflection. In this sense consciousness distinguishes itself from what might be called routine, habit, or automatic pilot: going through life's ordinary activities in the same mindless mechanical manner, reacting to similar situations in the same way, and doing so without the feeling and energy that participates in the new creation which each moment is.

Consciousness is active. It involves mindfulness. It involves perspective. It involves feeling. It involves sensitiveness. It involves being. It involves intimacy. It involves knowing. It involves direction. It involves expression. It involves free choice. It involves an awareness of our inner essence, as this inner essence is reflected in each of our situations, moment by moment.

It is in this sense that we can speak of a higher level consciousness, or an expanded consciousness. Higher level or expanded means a constant involvement in the living presence of the unity that is all. In this level of consciousness, logical inconsistencies can be held in unity. Events are not random. Everything that happens has pattern, meaning, and unfolding. There is joy, there is bliss, there is an intimate bonding with situation, with circumstance, and all people.

Everything is understood. There is immediate knowledge. The understanding is not linear, not cast in language, and not even thought about. For to think about it, is to bring it lower and objectify it. To cast the understanding in language is to make it linear. The language is description. The consciousness of which we speak is not a consciousness of description. Description addresses appearance. Consciousness not only addresses appearance, it addresses essence: the experience of the eternal now in complete unity – physical and spiritual, each person with the other, the consciousness of being and participating in the living presence of the Holy One of All Being.

It is in this participation that we change and move ourselves out of the box of our limitations. We become more sensitive and creative, more compassionate, loving, courageous and more fully connected to the present moment. We become more completely aware, watching and letting circumstances be, yet participating in them and taking responsibility. When we are more conscious, we perceive more possibilities for interpreting and acting in our situation. We become more effective. Inside we are mentally quiet, full of feeling, and without any negative emotional ego reaction.

Then that moment of expanded consciousness fades and we actively have to prepare ourselves for the next moment.

How do we prepare ourselves to participate in the next moment of expanded consciousness? To understand this, we must understand what in us limits this kind of consciousness. And although there are infinite varieties of limitation their pattern is similar. We limit expanded consciousness by selfishness: by our feelings of negative and destructive emotions, by our actions of vice rather than virtue, and by being too lazy or fearful to live consciously.

Think about it. Our negative and destructive emotions and actions of vice all make a separation. There is self and there is the other. Our feelings toward the other are negative. We are pushing them away with anger, arrogance, hate, lust, or impatience. We are not treating them as holy, we are not thinking of them as holy, so we can cheat them, dominate them, take advantage of them and so on. To increase our moments of expanded consciousness means that we must decrease and eliminate our moments in negative and destructive emotions, decrease and eliminate our actions of vice. And as we decrease and eliminate the negative, we must increase the positive emotions of loving kindness, fortitude, humility, and increase our positive actions of doing that which is worthwhile for us and for all. In this manner we draw everything towards us and unify ourselves with all.

The question is how to decrease and eliminate our moments in negative and destructive emotions. We are in a situation and for whatever the particulars of the circumstances, we discover that we are experiencing a negative emotion towards someone in the situation. The time for expanded consciousness is just then. But to get there, we have to make a change in ourselves. Our negative emotion is due to a negative judgment that we made. The negative judgment that we made was made because that other person did something to us that we judged as not for us. We are in the situation and we interpreted what happened as being against us.

Consistent with this interpretation we made our inner most being identify as the receiver of the action that was interpreted as being against us. But our inner most being is not just the receiver of the action that we interpreted as being against us. Our inner most being is the conscious agent, not only aware of what is happening but the writer of the lines and actions of our body's response. Consciousness is not just passive. It is active as well. Active means being open. Being open means being open to internal change and growth.

Nathaniel Branden writes:

> Living consciously is a state of being mentally active rather than passive. It is the ability to look at the world through fresh eyes. It is intelligence taking joy in its own function. Living consciously is seeking to be aware of everything that bears on our interests, actions, values, purposes, and goals. It is the willingness to confront facts, pleasant or unpleasant. It is the desire to discover our mistakes and correct them. Within the range of our interests and concerns, it is the quest to keep expanding our awareness and understanding, both of the world external to self and of the world within.[1]

We can discover that the experience we are having is not the only way to experience the situation. An experience, is an experience and there is something to learn from it. We must be open to the evidence reality gives us. We must be open to the possibility that there is an error in our thinking and judging. We must be willing to correct any errors. Our energies should not be tied up in defending ourselves, or emotionally reacting, but in creating and designing what is the most beneficial giving response we can make in the situation. To do that we have to undergo transformation. We have to give up our negative judgment, give up our attachments to that which we are holding onto, give up our feelings of having been hurt, give up our ego involvement in the situation, and learn something about ourselves that we want to change. Then we can respond in the best way we can, to do the greatest and deepest good.

All this implies that we understand, acknowledge, accept, and believe that we have the freedom and capability to focus our minds or to not focus our minds. We have the freedom and capability to be mindful or to be not mindful. We have the freedom and capability to think and be effective or not to think and not be effective. We have the freedom and capability to strive for greater clarity or stay put in our laziness. We have the freedom and capability to bring to conscious awareness what we might be fearful of or let it continue to reside

---

[1]Nathaniel Branden, *The Art of Living Consciously*, Simon and Shuster, New York, 1997, p11.

in our unconsciousness. We have the freedom and capability to examine our own internal unpleasantnesses or avoid facing them and working through them. We have the freedom and capability to be more fully conscious and live life with constant inner growth, with excitement, enthusiasm, and amazement, with energy and with love.

The situation we are in calls for our response. Our energies should not be tied up in defending ourselves, but in creating and designing what is the most beneficial giving response we can make in the situation. To do that we have to be open to undergo change and transformation. We have to give up our negative judgment, give up our feelings of having been hurt, give up our ego involvement in the situation, and respond in the best way we can to do the greatest good. We have to go beyond where we were. We have to write the lines of the giver. We have to be open to transform ourselves and play our part as God's messengers.

This is how we enter an expanded consciousness and fully live consciously. We accept who and what we are and take responsibility for our thoughts, feelings, emotions, speech, and action. When reality reflects our limitations to us, we are open to change and inner growth. We can be assertive when appropriate and unassuming when appropriate. We act with purpose, authenticity and integrity. This is the way we go beyond where we were. We write the lines of the giver. We transform ourselves and play our part as God's messengers. This is the process how we enter an expanded consciousness, God consciousness. We are fully living consciously.

Emotions

Emotion literally means to move out. The first letter *e*, is from the latin *ex* and is a prefix meaning out and the remainder of the word is motion, which is to move.

What is moved out is what is in our consciousness. Our consciousness holds our intentions, thoughts, feelings, and our immediate awareness. When these are moved out, they are expressed in what and how we say and what and how we do.

Psychology's usage of the term emotion is narrow, centered on feelings that arise spontaneously and without conscious effort. Psychology pays particular attention to mental states of anger, fear, agitation and disturbance because it is these negative emotions that cause people problems and keep them from functioning effectively.

Our usage of the term emotion is broader and relates to its literal meaning of moving out what is in our consciousness: our intentions, thoughts, and feelings. When these get moved out, we say they are expressed. Express means to press out. We press out our intentions, thoughts and feelings into reality. As they get pressed out, they are imprinted into reality.

Positive emotions move us toward, harmoniously embracing the other, helping the other and in general being constructive. Negative emotions move us away, discordantly roughing up the other, hurting the other, and in general being destructive.

As a person feels, so he believes his situation to be, often not recognizing that in fact his actual situation may not be in accord with how he feels. This confusion in recognizing that there may be a difference between how he feels and interprets his situation and the actual situation creates difficult and unintended consequences for the person, especially when the emotions are negative, such as with anger, jealousy or hate.

The first step in transcending negative emotions is to intellectually admit that there may in fact be a difference between the inner emotional state and its interpretation of the situation and the actual situation. Once the admission is made, the intellect can use discipline to suspend judgment, essentially pausing and grounding the process of emoting, so that it can begin to explore other possible interpretations. For this exploration to yield fruit, meaning to be able to come to an interpretation of the situation that is consistent with the actual situation, the emotions have to be understood in terms of intention.

To understand emotions, we must understand how we come to intend what we intend, how we come to think what we think, how we come to feel what we feel. There are two processes that govern this. The first process begins with our intentions. What is our purpose? What is it that we want to experience and bring into our consciousness? From the sacred point of view, the answer is that we wish to bring God into our consciousness.

God consciousness is a consciousness in which all that we sense: see, hear, touch, smell, and taste is a manifestation of God's glory. Once we will this as our purpose, we can interpret every aspect of our immediate situation in these terms. This interpretation is what constitutes our thoughts. These thoughts then bring on the associated feelings; and the totality is our emotion which we then express.

The second process goes on simultaneously and in parallel with the first process. The second process is a process of resonance; resonance here means similarity. Anything experienced and lived in our past that is similar to our current situation, our current interpretations and feelings, constitutes a resonance. Automatically, what we felt and expressed in the past, now because of resonance, gets brought to the present reality where it exerts its power to be re-lived and re-expressed.

If these past emotions are positive ones, then they resonate with our current positive emotions, adding energy to them and we become uplifted into a happier, harmonious state of being as we express ourselves in speech and action.

If these past emotions are negative ones and we have not worked on ourselves to ground them out, then we become ego-reactive. Such negative emotions of the past which resonate with our current situation impregnates itself into our current situation and the second process becomes the dominant process by which we express our emotion. It may become so dominant that we become enslaved to it. In effect we become like a broken record repeating over and over again the same negative emotional outburst in similar situation after similar situation.

The purpose of studying the emotions is to free ourselves of resonating with anything in our past that was negative for us. We can ground such emotions by letting them free. We break our attachment to them and give them up. Often what is negative for us is perceived as negative because it brings itself against our ego. Fundamentally, however, what is purely negative for us, is without positive meaning and without higher purpose.

But how can there exist that which is without positive meaning and higher purpose? For whatever happens to us has the hand of God in it. And whatever God does is fundamentally good and with sacred meaning. So when we make a negative interpretation about something that has happened to us, the interpretation must be incorrect. In this case we must seek a perspective from which we can find a positive meaning in what we had regarded as negative for us.

Higher purpose means to express God's ways and to serve as God's messenger. The classic religious language states that the higher purpose is to do God's will. Kabbalistically, the teaching is deeper:

> Do His will as if it was your will that He may do your will as if it was His will. [1]

The teaching is not to align our will with God's will so that there will be a consequent reward to us in which God will make His will our will. Rather the teaching is that by aligning our will to God, we become consciously united with God. Then in our own finite individual way, what we do is right action, what we say is right speech, what we feel is right feeling, what we think is right thought, and what we experience is a sacred experiencing. In this manner God makes His Will our will. In short, what we live is a sacred livingness in which all that is around us is holy; all that around us is pure, because our perception of all that is around us is the glory of God's immanence.

In discussing the situation in which we come up short and miss right thought, right feeling, right speech, and right action, the classic religious language uses the idea of separation. We separate ourselves from God, by not treating other people ethically, respectfully and correctly, or by not treating the natural world that God makes with care and reverence. This separation is called sin. The one who is living dominantly in sin is called an evil person.

The classic religious language for the opposite of an evil person is a righteous person. Today, the word righteous embodies additional connotations and denotations, some of which are negative. Perhaps this makes it not as an appropriate choice of word as it was originally. Today perhaps a better word would simply be a decent person.

A decent person can be of any religion or non-religion, of any religious observance, and of any socio-economic status. A decent person can be politically liberal or politically conservative. The hallmark of a decent person is one who acts in all person to person interactions in accordance with Torah, constructively, ethically and morally correct, inwardly and outwardly, with compassion for others. The emotions of a decent person are positive emotions. The decent person is authentic, honest, treats other people respectfully and correctly and treats with care and reverence the physical reality in which he lives. The decent person does not unnecessarily judge other people, does not engage in petty arguments, and does not make power plays to dominate, restrict, limit, or put down any other person. The decent person is helpful, making sure that there is space for the other person to be. The decent person enhances the possibilities for the other person's expressions.

---

[1] *Ethics of the Fathers*, 2:4

A decent person is not necessarily God-conscious. However, a person who is not decent, cannot be God-conscious. A God-conscious person is necessarily decent.

Our general goal is to move ourselves into becoming as decent and God-conscious as we possibly can.

Our Reality

We live in two realities: physical reality and spiritual reality. Different people who are in the same physical reality will sense the same external reality. But they may interpret it or receive it in different ways and thereby create different spiritual realities.

In each moment, physical reality is the question God asks us. Spiritual reality is our answer. The carriers of the answer are our internal feelings and our external actions. The content of the answer is in the intention behind the action.

The whole constitutes a song with two parts. In one part, God calls forth and asks: Am I here? The second part either answers with delight: I recognize you, you are here. Or the second part answers with despair: I do not recognize you, you are not here.

Our answer is not just an intellectual answer, requiring an intellectual act of discrimination resulting in the simple statement: I recognize you, you are here, or I do not recognize you, you are not here. Our answer is full of intention.

If our full intention, heart, mind, and soul is to be with God and draw near to the Divine, then we will answer I recognize you, you are here. If our intention, heart, mind and soul is not fully to be with God and draw near to the Divine, then we will answer: I do not recognize you, you are not here.

The issue before us is always only of one kind: whether or not the intention behind our thoughts, speech, and action is to be with God and draw near to the Divine, or heaven forbid, the opposite.

Why is this an issue? Certainly not because of a question of its desirability. We would never question its desirability. However, it is an issue because we may not believe in the Song. This is called not having faith. Or, it is an issue because we may not will to be in a state of God consciousness. This is called idol worship.[1]

This makes the primary issue being what is our will. Do we will to believe that there is the Divine? Do we will to believe in the Divine Song? Do we will to have faith?

[1] What we see we take as primary. In effect we worship what we take as primary. So if we do not see God, we must see something other than God. And as this something other is primary, we will worship something other than God.

Authenticity

There are two modes of living. Each is important and the first depends on the second and the second depends on the first. They are intertwined and inseparable from life as a totality, yet each represents a distinct kind of living experience. In this respect, both are meaningful, but the first distinguishes itself by being ultimately or absolutely meaningful while the second is at most ordinarily useful. A person may live only in the second way and not achieve his human and spiritual potentiality for the first. Such a person has not lived. The first is a sign of genuine life, thus we can call it authentic; by way of contrast, the second we will call non-authentic.

Authenticity is a term we use to describe the rich and effortless meaningful experiences, experiences of Being. Experiences of Being are the natural and self-justifying kind of living experiences of delight which fulfill the I who lives. Experiences of Being are a direct involvement with reality of God in the world around us. The involvement is a special kind of involvement for it reaches through itself and touches the physical and spiritual worlds. The I who involves himself/herself in this way is not an ordinary everyday I, but he/she is an I who is open to the existence of God's world. He/she receives and accepts the world and its situations as God's world. In the experience he/she is not concerned about the abstract, but rather with the concrete reality as he/she possesses it; he/she gives to it and it gives to him/her. As he/she gives to it, he/she is giving to God. As it gives to him/her, God is giving to him/her. He/she is sensitive to the world and knows its goodness, for its goodness is God's goodness.

Authenticity is always personal, arising from the depths of human interaction. Thus when we speak of authenticity, we speak of the authenticity of the *I* using the first person pronoun as the name.[1]

The fundamental character of authenticity is its individual genuineness and trueness. It is in authenticity that I realizes and manifests I's own identity. From an outsider's point of view, we look toward I and say I chooses himself/herself by acting authentically, that is, from all the potential actions, I actuates what I is through the action. The time period of the action is not the finite time period of the action as we usually conceive of time in the matrix world. The time period is eternity. That is why I actuates what I is through the action.

[1] This means that when you read the word I, it is not the I of the first person pronoun. Rather I is the name of the person. The dual meanings created by using I as a name rather than a person create a constant reading tension between the meaning of I as a name of a person and the first person pronoun I. This tension helps the reader think about I in the third person rather than recognize and identify with I in the first person. This tension creates a transcendent resonance in the reader which when accepted and affirmed will lead the reader to an understanding of the authentic I beyond an analytic intellectual understanding.

In experiences of identity, I feels he becomes I as I really is. I's expression is an expression of the deepest most essential aspect of I. I reaches I's maximum potential during that moment. I apprehends that I has had a peak experience; I's reflective consciousness realizes that there has been a complete unity with respect to the way it interacts with I's apprehending unreflective consciousness. Everything that has characterized the interpretations and judgments of the interactions previously is perceived by the apprehending consciousness as being now characteristic of the experience of identity. I finds himself/herself and I steps out to claim the action as his/hers. I experiences a direct involvement with reality. I experiences a direct involvement with God.

The experience of direct involvement with reality and direct involvement with God can be likened to the relationship between the self and life-space. The self includes not only the physical body of I, but the entire organization of his feelings and percepts. It includes all the person's physical, emotional, mental and spiritual dimensions. The self understands I's identity in terms of the life-space in which I moves about. Life-space encompasses more than the physical and social environment described by the objective observer; it includes all knowledge, memories, attitudes, feelings and emotions of the individual. The life-space is the spiritual and psychic living region. We name it consciousness. Identity as the experience of direct involvement with reality means that I's present actions and feelings in actual reality correspond perfectly to I's life-space, to I's consciousness.

Being authentic means that the I is, in such a way, that I is in accord with his own human and essential spiritual nature. He is true to himself. He is true to God. The I transcends the condition and habit from his actions and the actions become an individual self expression, an expression from his soul; it is not the action which is authentic, but the I acting with freedom who is authentic.

From I's outer point of view of the matrix, I lives in a neutral or even uncaring world; this world is the outer reality, the matrix reality I must face. Ultimately I is alone in this reality. The ways and people of the world try to push him around; I is influenced to do and think things in a way which is alien. I feels I's own integrity questioned. Should I stand there and let the world do with I as it wants? Should the world make I another peg in society's complex matrix structure? Or will I become distinctive by stepping out and claiming I as an unique I, true and authentic, not having to face matrix reality, but being true reality. When I is true reality, I is authentic. The reality that I is when I is authentic is the reality of God. It is a reality filled with vibrant color. All is alive.

What does it mean for an authentic I to claim himself? Every authentic I claims himself by turning the staleness of the matrix present into a living freshness, a freshness that is associated with the closeness of God. He transcends what he is, transcends his previous understanding, transcends his previous judgments, striving above his status to be come reborn as the non-judgmental person he/she truly is. I claims himself/herself by claiming his/her Godly self.

I is authentic by full-heartedness and affirmation. This internal affirmation comes as an expression of I's character and personality which is over and above mere rational acceptance and acknowledgement. The affirmation comes from I's inwardness which is in effect stating: "This action is me, one for which I stand. This action is an expression of my soul."

Every authentic I is free. To be free means to do what one intends to do acting spontaneously. I does not submit himself to the environmental influences around him. I, as an individual, chooses his action by sincere full-hearted acting. I wills his acts and I does not feel restrained under some external authority. Rather, I affirms his will and feels inner strength. I feels this inner strength as his freedom, a strength beyond the matrix.

Spontaneity refers to a quality of action. An act is spontaneous when I acts effortlessly in a non-action – when I does without doing and then affirms and reaffirms and reclaims the act. The initial affirmation occurs in a jump. First it was absent, then all of a sudden it is there. Later, the affirmation can grow in depth by reaffirming the act again. When I acts with I's whole heart, sincerely, but not a forced sincerity, when I puts I into the action, when I reveals for what I stands through the action, when I partakes in the livid concreteness with his whole self, when I acts with his entire being, the act is spontaneous.

I's spontaneous actions are an expression which radiate from the center of his personal existence, his inner self, character, and inwardness. I lives freely by: actively relating to the world, living productively, and reaching his potential. I fully participates in his act and both the act and the I become dynamic and creative. The act becomes an expression of the character of the I and thus fulfills the I.

In order to be free and authentic, I must be sensitive to life. Sensitivity means that somehow each additional circumstance and situation in which I is, in some way changes him. A sensitive person has an expanding intensive consciousness of his environment. I can distinguish each change and in some way the difference matters to I. This expanding consciousness is in effect an expanding consciousness of God in the world. For the authentic I, the consciousness of God in the world that I had yesterday is not sufficient for today.

This quality of self change with each additional nuance of experience means that I continually apprehends his world. When I's consciousness reflects upon his past experiences, it seeks a comprehension of the world and his reflective conscious acts of understanding continually progress. I is open to existence and always is becoming. For the authentic I, this constant state of becoming parallels the name of God which can be translated as *I will be as I become.*

Openness to existence means keeping freshness in everyday living. To live one must be a fresh flower nodding its head in the wind. Openness might be compared with the approach which people use in creative problem-solving situations. If I acts only on past learning and conventional ways of doing things, some problems will never get solved. If I does not have the past experience of solving problems, I will be severely handicapped by complete lack of method and routine although his attempted solutions might very well be novel efforts. The creative I has infused his past experience into a general understanding in which new ways of approach and organization can easily develop. I has balanced his past learning with the newness of the present unique situation. Similarly the creative I, by being open to his existence, keeps a fresh attitude toward life and I becomes sensitive to all essential parts of life. Thus I's understanding continually expands; I's life-space enlarges, and I's individual world becomes deeply fulfilling.

Openness does not mean living in a new, different or novel way; frequently the best way to act or live is in a way which the I has previously acted. In such a case I's openness becomes repetition; I acts as he has acted before; however, the acting or doing is not merely mechanical doing-again, but it is a doing which is just as alive and dynamic as the first doing. In repetition I affirms the doing that had been done before. In repetition I keeps if not expands his full-heartedness, affirmation and appreciative passion towards that with which I became involved.

The authentic I's action is whole, complete and one. When the action is truly harmonious, it is entirely complete, that is, when the action is finished I can look back and say: "Everything which happened and everything that I did could not have happened better; the absence or addition of any minute detail would have destroyed its perfectness." In general, nothing can be added or subtracted without radically changing the oneness of the action, which is really a oneness with God.

The authentic I is the I who wears no mask, the I who lives deeper than his/her surface, deeper than the matrix. The authentic I is I who is I in truth and sincerity. He/she is: I who is shielded by no armor, I who can feel and express feeling, I who does not try to force other people to be different than who they are, I who does not try to force other people to act differently than how they act. The authentic I is an I who is receptive to give himself and to receive others. To receive others means to be able to affirm and accept the other's expressions and actions as expressions of who they are. It is such a complete receptiveness that even when the other acts in a way or expresses a feeling that I did not expect or would have initially preferred to be different, I transcends. I receives it, I touches it, and I loves it. The authentic I is an I who appears naked and open before God and thus an I who can communicate with Thou, whether Thou be God, people, the world or life itself.

For the authentic I, oneness, freedom, spontaneity, involvement, and intimacy are inextricably tied together. The unity in the purposive direction is the unity with God. The movement along the purposive direction is experienced as freedom. The successful travel and fulfillment of the purpose is the experience of authenticity. The form of the action is its spontaneity. The guiding force of the action is in I's involvement with it. The action is intimate. It is an expression of I in the realm of Truth.

The I who is non-authentic, is at best, non-authentic in the face of necessity. Eating, sleeping, and working are all necessary for the physical and psychical health of the individual. These actions can be done authentically and non-authentically. The I who goes about eating, sleeping or working in order to keep at the minimal level of aliveness is not authentic. The I who goes to work merely in order to earn money so that I has a roof over I's head, food in the refrigerator, and a little for some pleasure is barely living. Such an I misses the essence of Godly life. Seemingly this kind of I is concerned for I's welfare, but in actuality I's own welfare has been forgotten. This I's doing does not make him/her any more of a person; the doing at best keeps the status quo. I is not reborn or enlivened through I's action. I is just barely living, which means living in the matrix.

The matrix lattice structure of the world, the traditions, customs, culture, and conventions of society give everything a certain order. This is the framework of living which provides a basic necessity of life. But today, because our age is so complex sociologically, politically, and technologically, people become so involved in the lattice intricacies – the everyday routine of living and role playing – that spirituality is hidden from them.

One plane of non-authenticity is superficialness. The superficial is an outright denial of the I's individualness. I makes himself be what he essentially is not. Superficialness is the first characteristic of bad faith. If authenticity is characterized by being and becoming oneself and non-authenticity by not truly Being, then superficialness is characterized by being what one is not. It is a cover which surrounds and conceals the I preventing any direct complete contact with the reality of God in the other. This cover is the matrix.

Another plane of non-authenticity is the commonplace, the trivial. Here living has been leveled down to such an extent that all purpose has been lost. The existence of the commonplace is boring. It is like the gossip or talkativeness at a party or at the lunch table in which nothing is really said. It is speech which speaks because time is on hand and there is nothing else to do. The trivial passes the time away and the I keeps from being bored by occupying himself with the trivial. Frequently the I who lives most of his life in the commonplace will have a world-view similar to the aesthete in the first volume of Kierkegaard's *Either Or*. In the rotation method, unless the aesthete frequently changes one commonplaceness for another, his life becomes boring. This is liking sitting in front of the TV and constantly switching channels.

One example of a commonplace situation where a necessary act is done but it is done inauthentically is one where I might place a key in a lock and turn the key which then opens the door. When the door is opened, I's concern and dealing with the lock are concluded. In fact, getting inside the locked door may be so important that I forgets and leaves the key in the lock. The key and lock were only important in that they led to some other action; they had no meaning or importance for I in itself.

Contrasted to this, if we look at a child who has just been given a key for a lock, we might notice the child repeatedly opening and closing the lock just for the sake of seeing the lock open when the key is turned. There is no other action towards which his curiosity and fascination with the lock leads. The is similar to the curious teenager or adult who is fascinated by taking things apart such as cars, telephones, computers, disk drives, etc.

A locksmith who is fixing a lock may be authentic in his fixing of the lock. In authenticity, he is completely involved with the lock. He is completely attentive to it. His actions of fixing it is an expression of himself. However, the locksmith may also be inauthentic in his fixing of the lock. He is working in order to earn wages. He uses his talent just to fix the lock; otherwise he has no interest in it. This is the average kind of action one finds in the matrix everyday life.

The basic quality of existence in God's world is genuineness. I may look at the moon. The moon is more than moon. The moon takes on a quality of beauty. The beauty is an attractiveness that draws I to it and keeps I drawn in it. Once the moon is looked at in this authentic way, I does not want to take his eyes off the moon. I feels for the moon. And I feels the moon feels for him. There is an intimacy that the outside observer cannot understand. The moon has become a Thou for the I.

I may wash a car. I is taking action upon a thing. I is doing to it. If I is authentic in this action, then I is not a separate I dwelling in a particular place in space, but I is intrinsically linked with the action washing and the object acted upon, the car. Similarly, the washing is associated with the I as the I washing rather than you, he she, or the machine washing, and washing the car rather than washing the floor, the clothes or the sidewalk. The car is not something parked out by the sidewalk sitting alone on the street, but is parked on the street in close proximity to the I and touches the I as the I touches it in the action washing.

The experience of the authentic I in washing the car is not felt as the linkage of two entities, one of which is acting upon the other. For the I washing the car is not the same I who might drive the car or who bought the car. The I washing the car is intimately associated with washing the car and nothing else. The action washing the car becomes part of the I; the washing the car and the I become identified with each other in such a way that the I equals washing the car. We can ask: "Who is the I?" We hear the answer: "I is the one washing the car." The I is the action and the action is the I.

A situation as the one represented above would commonly be described as the I is full-heartedly washing the car. I throws himself into the act and becomes part of it. I does what he wants to do as I wants to do it. The I is harmonious in the action. There is no conflict, no anxiety, and no work. When the action is completed, I feels "good" for having acted. I affirms himself and the action as having belonged together.

No amount of planning ahead could have enabled I to act with such a harmonious integration in the act. I had to be himself and act spontaneously every instant as I washes the car. The washing the car is an exercise of I's freedom. I may have had all kinds of influences which could tend to make him wash the car, but in authenticity, I is the last and only cause of his action. By authenticity, I is free and independent.

I full-heartedly washes the car; he directs himself completely to washing the car. I participates directly in washing the car. The action to him is more than the act of washing the car. I involves himself in washing the car; the action has great meaning for him. I cares about the car and cleans it. He uses the soap and water with diligence, carefully removing every trace of dirt from the car. As I washes the car, I does not think of anything, the past, the present, or the future. I washes the car in the livid concreteness of the present. I passionately washes the car; I feels washing the car, thus, I is washing the car.

Time as the clock reckons it has no place in I's action. I may take as long a five hours to wash the car, yet I may feel it as only five minutes. Through directing his consciousness so completely on washing the car, I is conscious only of washing the car. The duration which I perceives is an inverse measure of the emotional intensity and attentiveness of his consciousness. I intensely concentrates on washing the car; he endures one event – washing the car – and that being so with such great involvement, I feels I endures only a moment.

I is sensitive to the car. He apprehends every means and nuance of appearance. I is open to everything the car gives to him. He very keenly perceives the bare presence of the car. Without this sharpness and sensitivity the presence of the car would be hidden. I would see the car as a car, but just as any car which belongs to I. However, when I is open enough to receive the car, when I is sensitive to the car, the car takes on a unique character. I calls the car "she:" " Her engine purrs as smooth as you will every hear." I looks at the washed car and sees every bit of its metal skin perfectly shine and reflect the light falling upon it. I starts the car, rather he starts her up and from those initial grumblings of the engine, I can tell if all the spark plugs are firing and whether the carburetor or timing is adjusted properly. The engine grinds and starts and the slightest noise I recognizes as the worn valves or weak springs etc. I drives her and knows how the car will sound and perform over any kind of road. I knows the inner nature of the car and what he can expect from it. I knows and understand the car.

The meaning of understanding and knowing implies uniting and relating in a reasonable and sensible way that which is sensed and perceived. The understanding may have been conditioned through previous cogitation and rationalization, but the present understanding is immediately apparent as the recognition of a color.

Understanding means to understand things in a particular order or a particular context. The order in which the world is understood is not inherently given in the world. For the outer world is as it is and works exactly as God has made it to be. It is I as I tries to understand it, to comprehend what already is, who sets up I's ordered system, I's coordinate system in which I can classify and categorize and judge. I creates his own context. I creates his own order. The order which I perceives the world as having is really the order which I himself/herself created as being. The order is a direct reflection of how I understands I, what I is, what I's world is, and how God acts in the world. The extent to which I does understand the order I creates and the extent to which this order has a correspondence to the way the world works, I will act effectively in I's environment. Ineffective behavior shows lack of such understanding.

Understanding is not a relative process: either I understands a given order or he does not understand. When I does not understand a given order, he cannot look at the given world and order it in the way in which someone else has. Understanding or knowing is not objective; that which can be abstracted from understanding is, but then because the abstraction is an abstraction, unless I himself can existentially relate to the world as the abstraction describes, I will not truly understand the abstraction. The abstraction is a reference to understanding; it is a means of communicating and is not something which is immediately felt.

I tries to understand the world. I's understanding culminates in an ordered set of judgments upon the things and ways of the world. Those things which are in harmony with I's understanding of I, I values. The "values" are an abstract representation of this understanding of I's structure as a person. In the abstract these values are that for which I stands. I affirms them as I continually re-grasps and re-judges them again to be of value. I finds that I loves anything in the world which exemplifies these values.

In each situation that I is in, I can make a judgment whether that situation is for I or against I, that is whether it is consistent with I's values or not consistent with I's values. In judgment, I cannot be authentic. Judgment puts I in the past. There is no transcendence in judgment. Judgement is judgement of good and evil. Only authenticity puts I in the present with an acceptance and affirmation of the situation.

When I understands the world and accepts and affirms it, I can love the world as the world is. This kind of loving has been described in mystic feelings. Peak moments of love are very similar to two kinds of "mystic feelings:" oneness or identification with reality by feeling or being everything which the consciousness perceives and the other being a peak distinctive affirmation of reality. In the first I so completely affirms, accepts, and assimilates himself into his environment that he feels himself inseparable from it. I becomes the not-self which I is. I loses himself in the world. The second "mystic feeling" is opposite the first. Instead of I apprehending reality through assimilation, I distinguishes himself from the world. The chair in which I lost himself in the first feeling of love remains a chair. I realizes it as a chair with its own unique beauty and foundation in the all-encompassing groundlessness of life. In both cases the feelings are of love.

In I's relationship with the car, I can understand the car; I can reach out to touch the car, the relationship borders on intimacy, but it can never truly be fully intimate. The car will never show understanding of I; the car will never return any of I's feeling in an observable way. The relationship can go only so far. The car can never sustain I in I's aloneness. It is close relationships with others, others who can be an I too, that fully completes Life.

The authenticity that I finds with another I is similar to I's authentic relation to "things;" the difference is that there can be two active participants in the relation. The relationship is a primary one and is characterized by a shared intimacy, a complete giving and receiving.

From I's inauthentic point of view, life in the midst of the matrix world is a cold structure. For example in the business world, the structure is capability, successfulness in making money and objectiveness in judging situations of profit. These criteria impregnate society. People do not want to express feeling because feeling is sensitivity, weakness. So they begin to tolerate hurt, in fact, they can become indifferent to it. They harden their hearts and soon begin not even to feel hurt. This is society's criteria for strength. Only coldness, hardness, insensibility and insensitivity are in the midst of the matrix world.

I knows his authenticity. He knows his heart is warm and gentle. He knows his heart is full of love. And I knows that this love can be tended and cared for by other people, other authentic I's. For this to happen there must be closeness and this closeness is intimacy. In the midst of the matrix world, there is no intimacy, but in transcendence of the midst of the matrix world, I can leap in and participate in the intimate human experience.

Intimacy is a relation of love. Love can be between two particular people; however, it is not exclusive involving only two people at any one time, but inclusive in being part of the totality of the personality and character of the I who loves.

In love between two people, two people give, share and identify with each other whether in a relation of friendship or romantic love. They trust each other perfectly and completely. Neither would do anything to hurt the other. And if one appears to do something that had the possibility to be regarded as negative to the other, the other would not even think of making such an judgment. The two people recognize each other as human people – imperfect – yet dignified in beautifulness and wonderfulness. They realize each other as a separate unique distinct I and they understand through active acceptance of each other's shortcomings, they affirm each other for what they are and forgive each other for what they are not. Whatever the two do together, they enhance the activity just by being present and taking part with each other. They live unto each other in a world of feeling and intimacy. They share and communicate, care and be concerned for, listen and forgive, affect and thus be affected, trust and are trusted. In this sense they are one with each other; they are harmonious.

But this oneness in intimacy is not oneness. Intimacy contains privacy for each I individually. Two people do not share everything. Intimacy involves identification, but not such a complete identification that the two become one person; the two remain two. Just as the I, who washes the car, and touches the car, can never become the car, so the I in intimacy remains integral to himself. With intimacy, each I is not alone.

The I in intimacy is sensitive. I is open for whatever the intimacy brings and can recognize its meaning. I can respond and answer I's intimate friend's needs because I is sensitive to them. The relationship is dynamic and each I rides the waves of the world up and down in the intimate interaction.

The closest and most developed form of intimacy is the intimacy of two lovers. Here the intimacy encompasses life commitment. Both people affirm each other so completely that they can live with each other in the world. This affirmation is the affirmation of the kind of person the beloved is. I loves knowing that the person I loves lives a meaningful life. I loves with admiration and respect she who has playfulness, purity, innocence, and intellect. I takes pride in her personal character, and character we know, exemplifies individual life values. The relationship is dynamic and each I rides the waves of the world up and down in the intimate embrace.

I's affection is his total affirmation and acceptance and trust in I's beloved. This affirmation is unconditional. I loves his beloved for what she is as well as for what she is not. The unconditional affirmation includes unconditional forgiving. I can fully accept and affirm she who is lacking. Though there may be differences at times, these differences are overcome through the trust and playfulness in the relationship. When the lovers are able to maintain their authenticity, they experience an indescribable delight, an indescribable transcendence. For each lifts the other higher and higher, closer and closer they come to God.

Aliveness

Rhythmic softness soaring with time,
Penetrating and greatly expanding,
So joyfully being and feeling.

Dancing beauty everywhere, delicate and touching,
A shimmering multiplicity of simultaneous symphonies
Sounding colors and sensitive patterns,
Which in each instance and repetition are unique.

Such magnificence,
Such significance,
That the entire uncanny cosmos
Is textured in each leaf and flower,
In each whispering brick, rock, and house.

Rhythmic softness soaring with time,
Penetrating and loosely expanding,
So joyfully being and feeling
That by each gentle action
We naturally and heartedly bless
God's subtle and momentous cosmos
Who is our aliveness and love.

Darkness and Light

The experience of not seeing the light is the experience of darkness. When the light is not seen, it does not mean that the source of the light does not exist. Nor does it mean that the source is not shining; nor does it mean that the light has become disconnected from its source, for the rays of light are always connected to their source. Rather, it means that the light does not reach the receiver of the light because something has occluded the light, something has gotten in front of the receiver preventing the light from arriving.

The source of the light is God. The receiver of the light on the level of awareness is our consciousness. The receiver of the light on the level of spirit is our soul. It is we who occlude the light. When our consciousness does not receive the light, we experience darkness.

Darkness, חֹשֶׁךְ, represents that which is an obstacle to us. That which is an obstacle to us is that in which God is hidden for the purpose of its revelation. To be hidden means to not be in our consciousness. The revelation of that which is hidden requires a movement from us.

A fundamental aspect of our spiritual dynamics is the blossoming forth of Godliness, the manifestation of Godliness, the revealing of Godliness. Blossoming forth means that which was not in blossom and did not necessarily have to blossom, does blossom forth. The manifestation of Godliness means that the Godliness which was un-manifest, manifests. Revelation means that which had been unrevealed becomes revealed. And that which is an obstacle to us is not the hiddenness of that which is un-manifest. Rather, the obstacle is the lack of our own movement for we had forgotten or did not realize that it is un-manifest or hidden for the purpose of its own becoming revealed.

Now every obstacle has it own openings and every problem contains its own solution.[1] And the opening of our obstacles is accomplished by our seeking of God. And when we seek God, when we seek the truth, we make operative:

> The openings of Your words illuminates, making the simpleminded understand.[2]

Rabbi Nachman teaches:

> For the illuminating word, i.e., the aforementioned words of truth, show him the opening. Thus the verse concludes: "making the simpleminded understand" – the simpleminded who are situated in

[1] Rabbi Nachman, *Garden of the Souls*, Breslov Research Institute, Jerusalem, 1990, p94.
[2] *Psalms*, .119:130

darkness and cannot see how to depart, will understand and see the openings from which to depart the darkness. [3]

When we seek the full truth, the complete truth as we can comprehend it on our own level, then the light of God which is enclothed in us illuminates the opening we seek. This is the meaning of:

The Lord is my light and my salvation.[4]

The Lord openest the eyes of the blind.[5]

Thus with the light that is enclothed in us, we illuminate the darkness חֹשֶׁךְ, the ignorance חֲשֵׁךְ, that which is dark, obscure or lacking חֲשׁוּךְ, and we dissolve the obstacle.

We might think that the problems, the strife and suffering we have at our workplace, with our neighbor, in our home, or in our country are the real obstacles. We might think that the things which may make us sad are the real obstacles. But these everyday problems with which each of us struggles only constitutes the garment of the obstacle. They, in and of themselves, do not constitute the essence of the obstacle.

Rabbi Nachman teaches that the essence of the obstacle, the darkness, חֹשֶׁךְ, is חֲשֵׂךְ, which means *holding back* or *withholding.* For the essence of each obstacle we encounter is our own holding back from serving God. That is, the difficulty we encounter we perceive as a difficulty precisely because we are holding back, because we are not doing all we could to reveal the Godliness we are called upon to reveal, the Godliness which is our unique mission to make manifest in the Kingdom of God.

Each person

must do everything he can and then God helps him.[6]

And we can know that this is true because we believe:

Thou openest Thy hand and satisfyeth the desires of every living thing.[7]

Thou openest Thy Hand, they are filled with good.[8]

---

[3]Rabbi Nachman, *Likutey Moharan*, Vol 10, Breslov Research Institute, Monsey New York, p22.

[4]*Psalms* .27:1

[5]*Psalms* .146:8

[6]Menachem Schneerson, *Sichos In English*, Vol 12, Sichos In English, Brooklyn, NY, 1982, p8.

[7]*Psalms* .145:16

[8]*Psalms* .104:28

This teaching puts a completely different perspective on the suffering and struggling and sadness that we sometimes have, that we experience, and that we see others experience. For it tells us that however real the suffering of our obstacles are, this reality is only the reality we experience when we hold back and do not utilize the openings provided for us. Thus the obstacles are, in fact, only the outward surface reality, the surface whose purpose is to hide and carry the essence which it enclothes.

Now, when we see the material physical surface as the total essence, our intellect interprets this reality as empty. And indeed material reality in and of itself is empty. Why? Because empty means devoid of God, meaningless.

But when we see beyond the surface, beyond the sufferings of our ego, of our heart, and of our body, beyond the suffering we see experienced by our neighbors and loved ones, we see that the surface is really just the clay material by which we form our spiritual reality. It is this clay which becomes our opening.

But why, we ask, why is it that suffering and sadness have to be? Why is it impossible for the beneficence of God to be manifested continually. Why is it impossible for us just to be always in the light and always be joyful. Surely a God who is good can arrange a creation for our delight and constant pleasure. Why do we have to struggle to work for a living? Why can't we have all what we want all the time?

If we think seriously about these kinds of questions, we realize that it is our nature not to want to lose what we have and to constantly desire more than what we have, no matter how good our condition already is. Our questions about why we cannot have all we want then must change to the question why does God create us to have a nature of forever desiring what we do not yet have or have not yet attained? Why is it that we can never be satisfied always wanting more than what we already have, no matter how good what we already have is.

Here we learn that because God creates us with free will, we have a nature that forever desires. For it would be absurd for us to have a free will that cannot be used. And when we use it, we use it to desire what we do not already have. What could be more natural?

Thus, whether our desires have a material orientation or a spiritual orientation, they are never satisfied. Each instance of not-being-satisfied makes us sad. No matter how much we have already attained or achieved, no matter how much we know, and no matter how much we have experienced, from the point of view of the present moment the past of this having is gone and has no presence. The past of this attaining is gone and has no presence.

But so long as we are alive, each current moment makes a free will. And with a new beginning we have a new situation, new desires, new work to do, new potential obstacles waiting at every turn, and new potential struggles.

Each current moment and situation flowers a new beginning. This is the meaning of:

> With a beginning, God created the heaven and the earth.[9]

Here Heaven is the place from which the Divine Light comes and earth is the place of clay, the place through which the Divine Light is revealed.

> Now, the earth was unformed and void. And darkness was on the face of the deep.[10]

The earth is the place having simultaneously the possibility of being formed into a receptacle of receiving heaven or formed into a receptacle of not receiving heaven. Its beginning state is a state of being unformed. And in this manner the earth is deep. The darkness being on the face of the deep means that there has been no forming yet. The potential of the earth to be formed had not yet been actualized.

> And the spirit of God moved over the surface of the waters. And God said: "Let there be light; and there was light."[11]

The waters here indicate that the earth does not have a fixed shape. Just as water takes the shape of its container, so the clay of earth has the potential to take the form we direct it to take. God hovering over the surface of the waters actualizes the potential of the earth to be formed. And when God said: "Let there be light" the light issued forth from heaven and shined upon the earth, bathing the earth in the completeness of the light. And this is how the light of God became enclothed in us.

> And God saw the light, that it was good.[12]

It is the light which brings all the beneficence of God from heaven to earth. It carries only goodness, only bounty, only abundance. Therefore, contrary to the implicit assumption in the question we earlier asked about why is it impossible for us just to be always in the light, we are indeed always in the light.

> And God divided the light from the darkness. And God called the light Day, and the darkness he called Night. And there was evening and there was morning, one day.[13]

---

[9] *Genesis* .1:1
[10] *Genesis* .1:2
[11] *Genesis* .1:2-3
[12] *Genesis* .1:4
[13] *Genesis* .1:4-5

The dividing of the light from the darkness makes possible the situation in which we can use our free will to occlude the Divine Light. There was evening first and then there was morning means that first there is the call of darkness, calling for the light to be revealed. For darkness is the sign by which we know that we are called upon to reveal the light. Then there is the morning when the rising sun shines the light, when the light enclothed in us reveals the Godliness we are called upon to reveal. One day means that this is what happens in each moment, in each situation. For with a beginning heaven and earth are created for us.

What does this mean? It means that the new beginning presents our free will with a choice: how to interpret the new beginning. How to form the clay so that it can become a receptacle to receive the light; how to form the clay making the light be revealed.

That is, it is our responsibility, by being the agents of God, to make manifest the Divine Light. We do so by our expression. Expression is an outpouring of that which has been pressed in. Our expression is an outpouring of the light which God has enclothed in us. By this expression we declare what we are. And our expression depends directly on how we interpret the new beginning.

There are two dimensions relative to our interpretation: rationality and faith. An interpretation constituted by all rationality and no faith is one constituted by material, psychological, sociological, and ethical values. This kind of interpretation will yield us many insights about the surface structure of the new beginning. But it will not yield the insight of its essence. So with this kind of interpretation we will express obstacles and then encounter the obstacles we express. We will be in darkness.

An interpretation constituted by all faith and no rationality will be driven by the magical and the miraculous. It will yield insights of the essence, but without the body of the rationality, there will be little means to bring about the miraculous. So here too we will express obstacles and then we will be disappointed when we encounter the obstacles we express. We will not see the miraculous. We will be in darkness.

However, an interpretation constituted by a balanced blend of rationality and faith, a blend which has the necessary element of cleaving to God, such an interpretation leads us to know what our actions must be. And when we express our actions, not only do we do all we can, but by doing all we can we open the situation for God's help. And with God's help in the situation, the situation blossoms and we see the miraculous happen.

> We thank Thee, ...,
> For Thy miracles which are daily with us.[14]

[14] Amidah Prayer.

The miraculous happens. The light of God, which is the essence of the new beginning, is revealed. The new beginning manifests its end completion and then gives birth to another new beginning. There is no struggling, difficulty, effort, or hard work and there are no obstacles.

There is a miraculous success. A success in ways that we may not even have anticipated, a success that may even surprise us. A success in which we know that the

> success is not due to ... [our] own efforts, but to God.[15]

There is a great joyfulness. But the joyfulness is not over the success. Nor is the joyfulness a joyfulness of our service to God. Rather, the joyfulness is a joyfulness over the revelation of Godliness by which we elevate the physical, a revelation of Godliness which in turn elevates us being closer to God and to knowing and loving God, and an elevation which glorifies the name of God.

[15]Menachem Schneerson, *Sichos In English*, Vol 12, Sichos In English, Brooklyn, NY, 1982, p7.

The Dark Side Of The Moon

When we encounter a situation,
In which by our doing,
We bring down Godliness into the situation,
The lightness that we reveal,
Manifests as the light reflected,
From the Front Side of the Moon.

When we encounter a situation having
Divine irreconcilable elements within it,
And we are able to accept this diversity and conflict,
As part of the Divine Mystery,
And by our doing,
We elevate Godliness into the situation,
Then the darkness that we reveal manifests
As the dark light emanating from the Back Side of the Moon.
For this part of the Moon
Can never be seen or rationally understood.

The Heroic Act

How can we receive and accept that which we feel is not acceptable? For example, how can we accept the death of a loved one? How can we accept people who are acting to destroy us? How can we accept people who have abandoned us? How can we accept people who we trusted and now turn on us or cheat us? How do we handle something that we consider bad?

The list can certainly grow a hundred fold. How can such a question be answered ?

There are contexts and there are contexts. There are multiple levels of contexts. At the context level that the situation is bad and unacceptable, there is no life-nurturing meaning. There is only negative meaning. But I and my consciousness are part of the context. In my consciousness are values, beliefs, habits, perspectives, ethics, emotions, and personality traits. If I keep the context level in the place that is not acceptable, and do not do something that substantially changes the situation, I will be holding onto something which eats at me from the inside. I will not be at peace. I cannot stand the injustice. And there is no way to change or convert the injustice to justice. That is why it is unacceptable. That is why I suffer.

So there is a saying that time heals. We may get involved with other things and spend less and less time thinking about the bad or the injustice. But the injustice just shifts from the conscious state to the subconscious state. So it appears that it is no longer bothering me. But then something happens that reminds me of the injustice. Some kind of a situation that has some similarity to the original one. It does not have to be a big thing. Consciously or subconsciously, we start to think about it, and all those past negative and reactive emotions get reignited. We feel and then act in ways that are similar to the original unacceptable situation. But the actions and feelings are actually not appropriate. For the little new situation is not the grave previous situation. So there is some disfunctionality and that makes things worse for us.

Suppose for the moment that we believe there is a Creator, whose force and presence are all throughout every situation. Suppose for the moment that our time in this life is to grow, to enable the eternal part of us, our soul, to grow. Suppose that part of this growth is to bring a greater Godliness or greater virtue into this world and that the Creator gives us situations that we are uniquely able to handle if we can change the contextual level on which we receive the situation.

Virtue does not come free. It is not easy. If it were easy we would not call it a virtuous action. If we change our consciousness so that the contextual level changes and we are involved but at a different level, everything is different. At the prior contextual level, the injustice and the suffering are unacceptable. But when we change focus to what is the *correct* action or what is the *spiritually correct* action and concentrate on what the situation calls for, or in what way does this situation call for us to grow or for us to change. Our experience can be different and our actions can be different and more effective in bringing Godliness into the bad situation.

This is what the Zohar has to say about bad situations.

> There is no light except that which issues from darkness, for when that *other side* is subdued, the Holy One is exalted in glory.[1]

In this metaphor, darkness means bad. Light means good. In the Zohar, the other side [sitra achra] means the side distinct from, and opposed to, holiness. It may be thought of as a metaphor for the forces of the unholy, forces which bring us a bad situation. A bad situation is one that we say is not for us. To subdue the other side means we go beyond ourselves and act in a way that brings light issuing from the darkness. When this happens, virtue and Godliness is brought into the world. The Holy One is, therefore, exalted in glory.

How can we go beyond ourselves. What is the proper thing that we can do? In a split moment we have to change something in ourselves. Our ego becomes no longer involved. Our ego is that part of us that is holding on to the suffering and injustice. And by holding on, it limits us. The act that we need to do is understood after we do it as the *heroic act*. But as we do it, we think of it as only the best act that we can do. In it our ego joins our consciousness in a joyous ecstasy. We transcend where we were. The injustice is grounded. The suffering is past. Neither is present. What is present is only upliftedness.

What is the changing? We might have to change a belief, a value, some aspect of personality or perspective. We have to change or reframe something that is part of our consciousness.[2]

What happened to the suffering and injustice. It is not that we just let it go. Indeed we do let it go. But we let it go not into a subconscious state. We let it go by not holding on to it; We freed it. It has no more spiritual existence for us. It passed out of existence! We let it go by changing ourselves and doing the act the situation calls for, by doing what God is calling us to do. Later we and others might recognize that the act was an *heroic* act.

---

[1]The Zohar, Volume IV, Maurice Simon and Pual levertoff, translaters, The Soncino Press, London, 1978, (184a) p.125.

[2]In psychology reframing is a way of viewing and experiencing events, ideas, concepts and emotions to find more positive alternatives. It was introduced by Aaron Beck in his cognitive therapy or cognitive restructuring in the 1960's.

Is the contradiction still there? If we go back to the original contextual level it would be there. If we stay in our new contextual level it is not there. Can we stay at our new contextual level and think back to the old contextual level? Yes. Do we understand the contradiction? Yes. Does the contradiction bother us? No. The contradiction is of no concern now or any time in the future. Have we received the situation that was bad, so full of suffering and/or injustice. Yes. But to receive, we had to transcend, we had to grow, and we had to act the *heroic act* that brings virture and Godliness into the situation.

This is what creates the light from the dark side of the moon, the side of the moon that cannot be seen and cannot be rationally understood.

Metaphysics

Internally and externally,
I act; I do:
From the unlimited horizon of all acts
I perform an act.
In the givenness of the performed act, I experience.
And if I focus my attention,
I can be conscious of the experience.

When the context of this consciousness is on the body,
Through which I act, the experience is self-limited.
When the context of this consciousness is on the underlying
Fabric of the totality in which the act occurs,
I experience the unlimited unity of it all,
The Unity of Being.

I think. I question.
I question the question.
I question everything.
I question the all.
My act of questioning the all,
Brings me to experience that the all is unity,
The Unity of Being.

Internally and externally I am led to the same place,
The Unity of Being,
Which I experience as an unconditional ultimate reality:
A Living Presence.

Whispering Silence

In peaceful silence,
I wonder and I ask,
Deep questions,
Having no words.
Then sometimes,
The whisper tells me what I am.

Says the whisper:

> The person I am is defined by my feelings.
>
> > So I am play,
> > I am power,
> > I am beauty,
> > I am passion,
> > I am delicate,
> > And easily hurt.

Is this all?
Surely there is more.

Says the whisper:

> The spirit you are is defined
> By the motivation,
> For being the person you are.
>
> > So I am love,
> > I am freedom,
> > I am creator,
> > And I am for me.

Says the whisper:

> Now hear the fluttering of your butterfly wings,
> Wings which can take you anywhere,
> Here or beyond.
> Hear them singing:

I have complete freedom to become,
Whatever person and spirit I choose;
I have complete responsibility,
For the choice I make.

Over and over they flutter and lyrically mutter and sing:

I have complete freedom to become,
Whatever person and spirit I choose;
I have complete responsibility,
For the choice I make.

So simple and deep is this understanding.
That becoming spiritually whole and complete,
Is life's meaning and being,
That the understanding appears and disappears,
As in awe,
I listen and I learn,
From the knowing whispering silence.

With Faith

The many is the darkness
By which the One can be concealed.

The many is the brightness
By which the One can be revealed.

By our faithlessness does the many
Become dark and meaningless,
For without faith, there is only the many.

By our faith does the many
Become bright and meaningful,
For with faith, there is only the One.

With faith

Our heart is a mirror
By which the Divine reflects inward.
And our heart is a projector
By which the Divine emanates outward.

With faith

The physical is the external manifestation of the One.
And the spiritual is the internal manifestation of the One.

With faith

Our thoughts are directed solely toward the One.
And our consciousness dwells solely in the One.

The Message

> Divinity created matter so that man, composed of matter and soul, may have a conception of it. It follows, therefore, that all matter may be likened to a parable by means of which Divinity can be understood.[1]

And how can Divinity, that which is constantly bringing everything into existence with truth, beauty, joy, and love, be understood? Only by the understander acting as close as possible to the way the Divine acts: with truth, beauty, joy, and love, for the purpose of celebrating the holy. This is the message.

In order for there to be a message which is communicated, there must be the sender of the message, there must be the receiver of the message, there must be that which contains the message, and there must be the contents of the message. In a written message, for example, the container of the message is the letters by which the message is written. No amount of analysis of the shapes and geometry of the letters will uncover the contents of the message. The letters of the message are only the carriers of the contents, they are not the contents. Thus we say that the container conceals the contents of the message. The contents of the message can only be understood by a receiver of the message. And when the message is understood by a receiver, we say that the message has been revealed.

God is the originator of the message. We are the receivers of the message. Creation, physical reality, is the container of the message. That is the reason that if God were to stop the speaking the message, physical reality would cease to exist. And what is the contents of the message? The contents of the message is God. And where can we find God? Can we find God in the container of the message. Wherever and however we examine the container, physical examination will not reveal God. For physical examination only looks at the letters in which the message, that is, its contents, are written. Indeed, examination of any kind, can only look at the letters in which the message is written. Examination cannot reveal the contents.

So what does it mean that the contents of the message is God? Recall that the purpose of the message is for it to be received. And by being received influence, in some way, the receiver. If the message is God and we are its receiver, then it means that by putting God in ourselves, that is by receiving the message, we will be influenced. How will we be influenced? We will be influenced to spiritualize the physical reality. That is, we will be influenced to make this

[1] Louis Newman, *The Hasidic Anthology*, Charles Scribner's Sons, New York 1938, p. .83

physical reality a dwelling place for God. We will be influenced to do things in the most meaningful way.

As God sends us a message, we return a message to God. Our thoughts, speech, and action constitutes the container for the message that we originate. The contents of that message is the essence of our becoming. And when we make our physical reality a dwelling place for God, then the message we send is an echo of the message that God sends us.

This is the meaning that God is One.

Put Away Two

Put away two.
The world is One.

See One.
Hear One.
Smell One.
Taste One.
Touch One.

Seek One.
Know One.
Call One.
Feel One.

One is the first.
One is the last.
One is the singular.

One is the outward.
One is the inward.
One is the center.

One is going.
One is coming.

One is nowhere.
One is everywhere.

One is immanent.
One is transcendent.

One is All.

Control

With our great intensity,
We want certain things to happen.
We do things and say things
In our attempt to reach a goal,
In accordance with our will to control.

But actually the world is not that way.
We control what it is that we think, say, and do.
And even though what we do
And say and think has a direction
To achieve some kind of goal,
We do not control whether or not that goal is reached.
God has that control.

Therefore, we must shift the emphasis
From the goal to the pathway to the goal.
Make the pathway perfect.
If the pathway is perfect,
We have done all we could do.
Be happy.
We have done what the situation calls for.
We have done what God calls us to do.
The next move is God's move.
His move is always perfect.

If we struggle because the goal does not get reached,
Then we have lusted for the goal.
Lusting for the goal puts the goal ahead of God.
That means we engaged in idol worship.

The Ego

In ordinary language, ego refers to that aspect of self which our consciousness takes self to be distinct and separate from others and makes self be the center around which everything is organized. This usage is different from the technical definition ego has in psychoanalytic theory where it refers to that part of the psyche that functions as the organized conscious mediator between the person and reality. Spiritually, that which takes self to be distinct and separate from others, that which takes self to be the center of organization, is that which separates from God. And in this respect, it is a problem.

> Ego is the beginning and root of all evil. It is a mind process which separates man's consciousness from God-consciousness. It acts as a wall between man and God. The greater the ego, the thicker the wall.[1]

How can something which is as important as ego be such a problem? When the center around which everything is referenced is the self and not God, then the perspective from which we understand the world is limited. The more separate and distinct the self is functionally considered, the more limited is the perspective. And when we love with a limited perspective, the love is ego-directed to self. This limitation is too much. It is out of balance. There can be no transcendence. It is the source of the vices, the root of all evil.

---

[1]Randolph Stone, *The Mystic Bible*, (Beas, India: Radha Swami Sat Sang, 1956), p. .153

Ego Versus God Consciousness

To distinguish between the expanded state of consciousness that we call God consciousness and what might be thought of the limited reactionary state of consciousness, we call the limited state of consciousness ego consciousness. The principal property of ego consciousness, a property that runs through all its dimensions, is separation. Ego consciousness involves seeing oneself and everything else as separate from one another. This is the consciousness of the world as many diverse separate things and the many not relating to the Oneness that is. As a result, the experience is an experience of the good and the bad. By contrast, in God consciousness, the many diverse separate things of the world are all seen as part of the Oneness that is. As a result, the experience is the experience of the Good.

In ego consciousness, the world is experienced as objects. Everything in the world is an object to be manipulated, controlled, or transformed. The emphasis is on our having of the object and on our actions which manipulate and transform it. The experience of living in ego consciousness is an experience of maintaining our security and dignity through possession, power, goals, and control. Thus there is the superior and the inferior and we are constantly engaged in a selfish struggle to maintain, create, and hold onto what we regard as superior for ourselves, typically, for ourselves alone. Existentially, we become attached to our dignity and possessions and we lust for our goals. Our interpretation of everything is in terms of its appearance and not in terms of its essence.

In ego consciousness, the relevant verb is *having*. Because the relevant verb in ego consciousness is having, when we want what we do not have, we experience deficiency. And when we get that which we do not want, we experience deficiency. In deficiency, our emotional state is negative and we react. We push away those who have given us what we do not want. When our expectations are not met, we get angry and frustrated. We lose patience and become upset. We live in limitation.

By contrast, in God consciousness, the relevant verb is *becoming*. Because the relevant verb in God consciousness is becoming, each moment is complete, a miraculous and eternal now. We live in fullness.

The difference between ego consciousness and God consciousness begins with our internal values and our discipline in living. With God consciousness, discipline in living constantly pushes us to grow and transcend ourselves. Our values and beliefs are in constant development. And it changes the way we see things. Changing the way we see things is not just internal, a trick of the mind. It is a deep Torah teaching that the way we see our situations affects and can change the very situations we see.

Three Worlds

There are three worlds: the real world, the spiritual world, and the magical world. Actually all the worlds are the same world but we see and relate to them differently. In the real world, everything happens, deterministic or probabilistic, consistent with the laws of nature and physics. The spiritual world is our inner world of first causes. It is here that we have some consciousness of the holy in other people and it is here that our free will resides. Our spiritual experiences create differences in our behavior and they affect the way we live and the way we interpret our situations. It is from the spiritual world that our living with meaning and purpose arises.

In the magical world our consciousness perceives that there is nothing that happens by chance and what does happen is distinctive in non-expected happenings, happenings that are possible in the real world but not in accord with the expected behavior of the real world. For the religious person[1], the real world is the magical world for it is in the real world that God is revealed in part by our thoughts, feelings, interpretations, and actions. The magical world is the world of awe and wonder and we feel a joyous ecstasy.

The issue is what is the discipline we have to maintain to be in the magical world? The first discipline is non-judgment. Non-judgment does not mean non-judgment in all situations. In certain situations we have to make choices relative to action. If we are going to act, making such choices requires judgment. But there are many situations in which we are and there is no necessity for action. In these situations we are not called upon to make judgments. Nevertheless, it is not uncommon for people to insist on making judgments.

Before a judgment is made, the situation has multiple simultaneously possible potential interpretations. The situation is not one nor the other. It exists in limbo and we can relate to it that way. However the moment we make a judgment, its limbo status collapses and we are confined to live the situation through, consistent with the judgment we made.

There is a large class of judgments that relate ourselves to others. These judgments can be relative to having or being. What is it that the other has that I do not have? A judgment of what the other has and I do not have sets up a spiritual deficiency in ourselves. We want for ourselves what the other has and

[1]Religious person here does not simply mean that one whose external behavior is in accord with the body of religious teachings that the person subscribes to. Rather it means that the external behavior and the livid internal consciousness are consistent with the body of religious teachings that the person subscribes to. The religious person in this sense is one who has God consciousness and uses his/her discipline to come back to God consciousness after falling away from God consciousness.

we do not have. What is it that the other does not have that I have? This sets up the sense that I am better than the other; I have more. Or what is it that the other has done to wrong me? This sets up the ego to grow and fight the tangle of injustices and retaliate. In either case the ego necessarily expands and the ways to heal what needs to be healed within us and thereby transcend the situation disappear. The opportunity to put holiness and harmony in the place of strife, the opportunity to return to the magical world disappears.

Notice that either of these kinds of judgments is something that is not required because there was no necessity for action. Feeling bad because of a perceived deficiency or injustice or feeling good because of a perceived sense that I am better than another or because I can retaliate arises only because we let our judgmental thought processes go on uncontrolled. The moment such judgments are made and nurtured is the moment that we lose God consciousness and is the moment we leave the magical world.

In the magical world things are always happening. But their happening is not because of our control. And when they happen, because we have not made prior judgments, their happening is unexpected.[2] We find their happening as interesting. We interpret their happening as the hand of God in operation. In the magical world, there is no need to dissect the situation and figure out why. In the magical world, we just live, feel, and experience the situation through and through. If there is the potential for us to act, we act, within reason, in accordance with what the situation calls for. Our action does not require us to ask the question "what is in it for me?" That question is not relevant. For what the situation calls for is what God is calling upon us to do. The situation is God's open door and blessing to us and what we do fulfills the blessing. And since there is no judgment that we are better or worse than another, our ego is kept in its place. Therefore, nothing in the situation gets us upset or angry. Because we have a sense of God's hand in the situation, we are delighted and we are amazed. What we do is not arrived at by scheming. It is arrived at by a pure heart supported by thinking.

How can we tell whether our magical world is an illusion or not? In an illusion, an expectation is set up that is in a direct contradiction to the possibilities that can happen by the laws of the real world or by the laws and ways of the culture in which we live. Thus when things happen and we take action, there are side consequences. For example, if in our magical world we have a sense that we should get an unsecured loan with good interest rates. And we look on the internet and find a possibility whose interest rates are as good as secured loans and the protocol involves sending the lender money in advance for the

[2]Unexpected not because we had made a prior judgment that it would not happen, but unexpected because we did not make any prior judgments.

work of setting up the loan, we are in illusion and not in a magical world. In the real world, unsecured loans do not get an interest rate as good as an secured loan and honest borrowing institutions will never ask for money ahead of time. What money they require for setting up the loan will come out of the amount of money they provide for the loan. Thus the situation we think is in the magical world is actually an illusion. If we send money, we will lose it. For we have simply been sucked into a scam.

If in our magical world, we hold that the real world justly owes us something for whatever good reason, and we get angry or frustrated because we are not receiving what we believe the real world owes us, we are in illusion. For our family or the real world owes us nothing. It is we who owe the real world something. We pay what we owe by our service and by our work in the real world that yields results. If we want money, we have to do ordinary work to earn ordinary money. We have to take full responsibility for ourselves and our well-being. The real world owes us nothing. In short, if we in our magical world are not acting responsibly and are not getting results, we are in illusion.

The magical world can include all that is possible, including out of the box stuff, that could occur in the real world. But it cannot include that which is absolutely not possible in the real world. We can tell our magical world is not an illusion by our effectiveness. In the magical world, our actions are effective and they do not carry side consequences with which we have to attend to later. We can tell because we are able to maintain a state of well-being without upsetness. In the magical world we can maintain a state of radical amazement because our living is a living prayer.

Daily, we can call upon God to help us change. There are many kinds of prayers. Here is one:

Dear God,
Holy One of All Being,
I Bless You with all my heart,
With all my Soul,
And with all my Everything.
I am thankful for your daily miracles
And for all that you have given us.

Help me grow and change.
Please spiritually uplift,
And help me transcend where I am,
So that all life nurturing and beneficial energies
That I form and transmit
That affect me, others, and my environment,
Increase and be enhanced.
And all life starving and detrimental energies,
That I form and transmit,
That affect me, others, and my environment,
Decrease and be diminished.
For now and into the future
For as long as appropriate.[3]

Thereby help me think, feel, and create
A Perfect Rhythmic Balanced Interchange,[4]
In all that my life touches.

With deep gratitude,
Thankyou for receiving my prayer,
I remain Your loving child,
(Here put your name.)

---

[3] Some of the phrases in this prayer are motivated by the form that Joey Korn's prayers take in his work, petitioning God to increase beneficial energies and decrease detrimental energies affecting the environment that a person lives in. Joey Korn, *Dowsing A Path to Enlightenment*, Sugar Creek Press, Grovetown Georgia, .2013

[4] This is Walter Russell's phrase.

Encountering

We encounter.
And often without thought,
We interpret.
And take what we interpret to be true meaning.

But true meaning is always a unity,
Of what is sensed in the encounter,
And what framework we employ,
In making our interpretation.

Change the framework,
And change what we take to be true meaning.

What we sense in the encounter,
Simultaneously has multiple potential meanings.
If we choose any one of the narrow frameworks,
Concerned with self alone,
We will be more judgmental of others.
And our meaning will be characterized
By separateness and exclusiveness.
We will be leaning toward or manifesting vice.

If we choose a more global framework,
We will be less judgmental of others.
And our meaning will be characterized
By connectedness and inclusiveness.
We will be leaning toward or manifesting virtue.

One way turns toward and connects with the other side.[1]
There we experience multiplicity and turmoil.
And we burn with a hot fire.
This is Death.

The other way turns toward and connects with Godliness.
Here we experience unity and tranquility.
And we glow with a radiant light.
This is Life.

---

[1] In Kabbalah, *other side* is a code phrase of the unholy.

On Identity

What I am,
Is the meaning of the intentions,
Behind my actions.
Thinking, Feeling, Acting, and Saying
Constitute my freely chosen acts;
These are my powers of being;
They are the ways in which
I physically create my internal and external world.

At each moment in time,
As I become,
By exercising my powers of being,
I have a purpose,
I have an intention,
Which I assert.

This purpose and intention,
Is not merely to do what I do,
Is not merely to feel what I feel,
But it is an assertion of some aspect,
Of for what I stand.
It is an assertion of how I wish to creatively be.

What I am is not the actions themselves,
But it is what my spiritual being,
Intends to accomplish,
Intends to create by their existence.
It is an assertion of a symbol from the labyrinth
World of symbols in which my spirit lives.
It is an assertion of the spiritual being I am.

From this framework,
What I hold to be worthwhile,
What I hold to be good,
Are the intentions and purposes,
I consistently and repeatedly assert.

Who and what I am,
The identity I choose to be,
Is the total meaning,
Of the intentions and purposes,
That I hold to be worthwhile.

Cleaving

> *And Ye who did cleave unto the Lord your God, are alive, every one of you, today .*[1]

On this verse the Zohar teaches:

> The children of Israel stand here below as emissaries of the Most High, to open the gates, to shed light upon the ways, to kindle the radiance of the heavenly fire, to draw all things that are below near to them that are above, in order that all may become a unity. Therefore it is written:[2]

> *And Ye who did cleave unto the Lord your God, are alive, every one of you, today.*[3]

---

[1]Deuteronomy .4:4

[2]*The Zohar*, Vol 4, (II, 181a), trans. Maurice Simon and Harry Sperling (London: Soncino Press, 1978), p. .115

[3]Deuteronomy .4:4

Two Tortoises, A Well and The Sea

Once there was a tortoise living in a well, where another tortoise came from the sea. The tortoise of the well questioned the other as to the extent and size of his sea. The other replied that it was very vast. The first tortoise just made a leap and inquired if the sea was so big; and got the reply that it was much bigger. He made another leap and inquired again, and then another jump, and so on, till he completed the whole circuit of the well; but was invariably given the same answer. The poor tortoise of the well was at its wit's end to understand this, for he could not imagine any water to be bigger than *his* well. At last he said to the other:

> There is no such thing as the sea. You are telling a lie, or you are under a delusion.

The tortoise of the sea simply laughed at the folly and narrow mental vision of his companion, and kept quiet; for he could not prove his point to such an obstinate and blind fellow.[1]

---

[1]Lehk Raj Puri, *Mysticism, The Spiritual Path*, Vol I, India Offset Press, New Delhi, 1986, p .60-61

Kabbalah

The word Kabbalah is the English transliteration of the word Hebrew word קַבָּלָה,which means *receiving, receipt, reception, acceptance* as well as *oral tradition.* The teachings of Kabbalah tell us how to fully receive the bountifulness that God is continuously giving us. And by receiving this bountifulness, we will draw nearer to God. Thus the teachings of Kabbalah constitute the soul of our traditional religious teachings.

The root from which the noun קַבָּלָה comes is קבל, meaning to *receive, accept,* or *take.* We must understand that each situation in which we find ourselves is a situation that God gives us. Because it comes from God, each one has an inherent goodness within it. Our job is to fully receive it by acting in that Torah correct way in which this inherent goodness can be completely revealed. When we do so, we fulfill the mitzvah:

> *You shall be holy: for I, the Lord your God, am holy.*[1]

It is not so easy to do that which can bring out the inherent goodness in each of our situations. Our difficult situations are hard to receive. For to fully receive them, we must go beyond where we are, we must transcend our limits, moving to the next level of being who we are.

Our moment to moment situation and all the people in it is what God gives us. This is God as the lover and we are the beloved. The situation calls for a response. In responding by thinking, speaking, feeling, and acting in a Torah correct way, we become the lover and God the beloved. By so doing, the letters יה unite with the letters וה of the Divine name. And we get a glimpse, a momentary sense, of the Divine. This is how we proclaim or call upon His Name. Here calling means inviting. Our Torah correct response calls and invites God's presence to reveal itself to us and this is the glimpse, the momentary sense, we have of the Divine. Here we feel loved and give thanks to the Lord.

If we ourselves are deficient in that our thinking, speaking, feeling, or acting is not Torah correct, from our point of view the letters יה do not unite with וה. God remains completely hidden from us. We have stress or distress. Nevertheless, God completely receives our deficient response and in love sets up for each of us our future situations designed precisely to help teach us and give us the opening we most need to be able to learn to respond in a Torah correct way.

We can learn more about what it means to receive by referring to scripture. The word וְקַבֵּל is the second person masculine singular Piel imperative with conjunctive prefix of the root קבל (קַבֵּל). It occurs in Proverbs.

---

[1]Leviticus .19:2

> *Hear counsel, and receive instruction, that thou mayst be wise in thy latter end.*[2]

The word translated as instruction here is מוּסָר. It carries the additional meanings of ethics and morals. So paraphrasing the verse in Proverbs, we must listen to each situation and receive the Torah ethics and morals it is intended to teach us so that our doing will make us wiser.

The Torah ethics and morals referred to here must be coupled with the notion that we must go beyond our current limits. Our doing must not just be Torah ethically correct. It must strive to be an exemplar of going beyond the call of duty that might be expected by Torah ethics. For our doing is our service to God.

This can be said in another way. Our difficult situations are difficult precisely because they are the openings God gives us by which we can manifest virtue. And in what situations are the deepest and strongest virtues manifested? When the situation is easy? Obviously not. The deepest and strongest virtues are manifested only when the situation is difficult. So if we are to be what we truly are: becoming holy, then we must have our share of difficult situations in which we have the opportunity to manifest the strength of our virtues.

Hebrew is a holy language. Language patterns and relationships in Hebrew are not by chance. They all have spiritual meaning. There is another root with the letters קבל.The root קבל (קָבַל) means to *complain* or *cry out against.* Why are there two roots with the same letters one having a meaning to receive and the other to complain? Because there are two spiritual ways to relate to living: one way is to receive all that God gives; the other way is not to receive all that God gives. And if we do not receive all that God gives we will complain. We will cry out against God.

It is exactly this kind of issue that Job deals with. After all of Job's wealth was taken from him, he was afflicted with vile sores from the soles of his feet to his crown. And his wife said to him:

> *Dost thou still retain thy integrity? Curse God, and die. But he said to her. Thou speakest as one of the foolish women speaks. What? Shall we receive good at the hand of God and shall we receive not the evil?*[3]

Job's wife would rather not receive and, therefore, complain about his bad fortune than receive it. Job is saying to his wife that everything that happens to us happens by the hand of God. Some things have the appearance of good. Some things have the appearance of bad or evil. But whether the appearance is good

---

[2]Proverbs .19:20

[3]Job .2:10

or the appearance is bad we must receive it. Here Job uses the verb נְקַבֵּל,which is the first person plural Piel imperfect of the root קבל, meaning to *receive*. This is Kabbalah: receiving.

God gave these teachings to Moses on Mount Sinai. They were passed on orally, generation to generation, to those people on a spiritual level ready to understand and live it.

Those people who are not on a spiritual level ready to understand and ready to learn to live in accordance with the teachings of Kabbalah will find the teachings confusing and incomprehensible. For them the teachings will make no sense and even appear to be contradictory to traditional Jewish religious teachings. But there is no contradiction. It was because of this possibility for misunderstanding that the teachings were orally and privately transmitted only to those people who were ready for it.

There are many spiritual, mental, emotional, and physical facets to receiving the bountifulness that God is continuously giving us. We begin learning about them by first learning the meaning of Kabbalah, receiving. For this we will consult the Torah, reasoning in an associative way, rather than in the logical linear way our western education has trained us. In this mode, the linear logic is not completely expressed, precisely for the reason that the level of understanding which we seek does not have a complete expression. This level is the level of wisdom, the level on which the foundation of the world is built. And this is the first and highest level for which we can have a conscious recognition of the meaning of the receiving that Kabbalah is all about.

One way to read Torah is chapter by chapter, story by story. This kind of sequential reading opens us to receive on one level of understanding. The sequence of one verse following another as in a story provides the thread that holds this kind of understanding together. The resulting understanding is more of a finite or closed understanding. To associatively understand, we read one verse and another, but these verses are not in sequence. What holds them together is the linkage of their contents. The resulting understanding is more of an unlimited or open understanding.

The gematria of the word קַבָּלָה is 137: 100 for ק, 2 for ב, 30 for ל, and 5 for ה. We will find in Torah words having gematria of 137 and we will understand קַבָּלָה through the verses in which they occur.

The word בְּקֹלָהּ is the only word in the Torah that has the same letters as קַבָּלָה and therefore, has the gematria of .137 It means *unto her voice*. It is a word that God uses when talking to Abraham.

In all that Sarah saith unto thee, listen unto her voice.[4]

[4]Genesis .21:12

From this we learn that to receive we must first listen, for there is always something to be heard. Listening here is not listening to the chatter of various thoughts passing through our minds. Listening here is listening to the Matriarch Sarah, the one whose level of prophecy was even greater than Abraham's. The Sarah to whom we listen is the Sarah within us, for each of our souls has a facet of each of the biblical personalities.

The word בְּפִיהֶם has the gematria of 137 and means *in their mouths*. It occurs exactly once in the Torah. When God tells Moses he will soon be returned to his forefathers, He tells Moses to recount the teachings to the Israelites. He says:

> *Now, therefore, write this song for yourselves, and teach it to the children of Israel. Put it in their mouths, that this song may be a witness for Me against the children of Israel.*[5]

Our mouth constitutes the opening in our bodies through which we put food. The food nourishes us. It provides us sustenance. God is telling Moses: Put these teachings in their mouths through their openings. Draw these teachings into their bodies that the children of Israel may be spiritually nourished. Draw these teachings into their minds that the children of Israel may be always conscious of them so that they may dwell in the land of milk and honey.

These teachings will be a witness for Me that I have explained how to live in the land of milk and honey and I have explained the consequences of not choosing to live in the land of milk and honey.

The word מוֹצָא means *that proceeds out of*. It has the gematria of .137 God uses this word in speaking to the Israelites.

> *All the commandments that I command thee this day shall ye observe to do, that ye may live and multiply and go in and possess the land which the Lord swore unto your fathers. And thou shalt remember all the way which the Lord thy God that led thee these forty years in the wilderness that He might afflict thee, to prove thee, to know what was in thy heart, whether thou wouldest keep His commandments or not. And He afflicted thee, and suffered thee to hunger and fed thee with manna, which thou knowest not, neither did thy fathers know; that He might make thee know that not by bread alone doth man live, but by every thing that proceedeth out of the mouth of* יהוה *(HaShem) doth man live.*[6]

This is a direct statement telling us that the food which enters our mouths and nourishes us are the words which come out of the mouth of God. It is these

[5]Deuteronomy .31:19
[6]Deuteronomy .8:1-3

words by which creation continuously is. It is by these words that the spiritual life inheres in the physical world. It is to these words that we must listen. And these words come to us through our ordinary daily situations.

The word וֶאֱמָץ is the Kal imperative second person masculine singular with conjunction of the root אמץ, which means to *be strong, vigorous, bold, valiant*, or *of good courage*. It has the gematria of .137 Moses uses this word when he speaks with Joshua, preparing Joshua to take over the leadership of the Israelites.

> *And Moses called unto Joshua, and said unto him in the sight of all Israel:*
>
> > *Be strong and of good courage; for thou shalt go with this people into the land which* יהוה *(Hashem) hath sworn unto their fathers to give them. And thou shalt cause them to inherit it.*
> >
> > *And* יהוה *(HaShem): He it is that doth go before thee. He will be with thee. He will not fail thee, neither forsake thee. Fear not, neither be dismayed.*[7]

When we receive, we can be strong and of good courage, even if the situation is difficult, having the appearance of bad or evil. For by receiving we enter the land of milk and honey, the land that God has given us. This is our spiritual inheritance. Do not worry about the difficulty. For יהוה, HaShem, has gone ahead of us. That is, יהוה has arranged just the right circumstances that provide openings for us that we may ascend spiritual level upon spiritual level. God will be with us. יהוה will not fail us. יהוה will not abandon us. We need have no fear. We need not be dismayed. What God gives us is exactly at the moment that we can handle it and by handling it in the Torah correct way we elevate ourselves one step closer to becoming holy.

The word וַיְחַבְּקֵהוּ also has the gematria of .137 It means *and he embraced him*. The Torah uses this word at the time that Jacob is about to meet his brother Esau after being apart from him for many years.

> *And Esau ran to meet him, and he embraced him and fell on his neck, and kissed him; and they wept.*[8]

Here we learn that it is in the difficult circumstance that we will meet our Esau. Esau stands for that in us that is animal-like, that which in us is far from God. By fully receiving what God gives us in our situations, we can have even

---

[7]Deuteronomy .31:7-8

[8]Genesis .33:4

the animal part of us embrace our Jacob, who stands for that in us that is close to God. This embracing is a unification of the near to God essence with the far from God essence.

The word וְנַעַבְדָה is the first person plural Qal cohortative imperfect with conjunctive prefix of the root עבד, which means to *serve*. It has the gematria of .137 The first time it is used in the Torah was when the Israelites had just left Egypt and they were by the Sea of Reeds when they saw the army of Pharaoh marching after them. There were some among the Israelites who said:

> *Is not this the word that we spoke unto thee in Egypt saying:*
>
> > *Let us alone, that we may serve the Egyptians.*
>
> *For it is better for us to serve the Egyptians than we should die in the wilderness.*
>
> *And Moses said unto the people:*
>
> > *Fear ye not. Stand still and see the salvation of* יהוה *(HaShem), which He will work for you today. For whereas ye have seen the Egyptians today: ye shall see them again no more forever more.*[9]

The Egyptians stand for our limitations. To serve the Egyptians is to serve the limitation in us. In the difficult circumstances of having to face the possibility of fighting the soldiers and chariots of Pharaoh, there were some among the Israelites who thought the situation was impossible. That there was no way out. Therefore, it was better for the Israelites never to have left the bondage of Egypt, never to have left the limitation and constraint of Egypt. But Moses says: Do not fear. Stand still and receive. See the salvation. For that level of limitation which binds you and which you see as pursuing you, you shall see no more.

In effect Moses says to the Israelites, there is a way out. The way out is not logical. It is not a way that you control by purely rational means. You need not cry out. You need not fight. In this situation you even need not pray. Just let God do what needs to be done, through you. Do the Torah correct action, an action which is beyond the acts of where you have been. When you do, God will make a miracle. The Sea will split and you will walk through. That limitation that you have gone beyond will be left behind. You will see your Egyptian taskmaster, the taskmaster who kept you bound to your limitation, dead in the Sea.

Again the word וְנַעַבְדָה is used in the section of the Torah describing false prophets, what prophets and people not to listen to.

---

[9]Exodus .14:12-13

If in secrecy thy brother entice thee, the son of thy mother, or thy son, or thy daughter, or the wife of thy bosom, or thy friend, that is as thine own soul, saying:

Let us go, and let us serve other gods,

gods that thou hast not known, nor that thy fathers have known, the gods of the peoples that are round about you, those nigh unto thee, or far off from thee, from the one end of the earth even unto the other end of the earth, thou shalt not consent unto him, nor hearken unto him. Neither shall thine eye pity him; neither shalt thou spare; neither shalt thou conceal him.[10]

This second verse having the word וְנַעַבְדָה is yet stronger. Whatever in us that urges us to serve other gods, which means putting something other than God first, we are not to listen to or to pay attention. We have a choice to receive the situation God gives us or not to receive it. If we are enticed and do not receive, then it is equivalent to serving other gods. Other gods means idolatry. Idolatry does not mean only bowing and giving reverence to wooden statues. Idolatry means putting anything other than God first. Idolatry means having anything in our consciousness that is not connected with holiness.

We engage in idolatry when we engage our vices: for example, when we engage or activate self-satiation, anger, arrogance, lust, deceit, sloth, or avarice. These are the gods which we have not known. These are gods which our forefathers and foremothers have not known. These are the gods of the people around us. These are the gods on the non-God conscious we see people in the street serve. These are the gods that we see people on television serve. These are the gods we see some politicians serve. These are the other gods, the gods that throw us out of the land of milk and honey and into the land of limitation.

To summarize what we have learned about קַבָּלָה, receiving:

- We must receive our situations and reveal the possibility of good it contains by doing the Torah correct action.

- To become wiser, we must receive the instruction within our situations.

- We must receive the easy and the difficult situation as the hand of God.

- Our difficult situations are openings to manifest virtue, going beyond the call of duty.

[10]Deuteronomy .13:7-9

Scripture tells us to listen unto the voice our our Matriarch Sarah. This is that part of Sarah that is within us. By listening we will be able to receive that which God gives us and we will be able to put it in our mouths so that it can nourish us. What God gives us proceedeth out of His mouth. These are the words God speaks by which everything is and comes to be. Our experience of this is in the moments of our everyday situations. Our doing that manifests virtue must be a strong, vigorous, valiant doing. By this doing, we embrace our situations and we do not serve limitation. Rather through our Torah correct doing, we grow and transcend ourselves reaching for higher and higher levels of service to God. And by this way we move ourselves in the direction of holiness.

Become Holy

The central mitzvah of the Torah is

Be holy for holy am I, Hashem[1] your God.[2]

One interpretation of this verse is that just as God is holy, everyone has the potential to carry holiness. Therefore, we must treat each other in ways that recognize the holiness that is being carried.

But there is a deeper meaning when we translate the Hebrew in a way that explicitly recognizes that the verse in Hebrew is in the imperfect tense, meaning an uncompleted action. In English an uncompleted action can be thought of as one that is being done in present but not yet completed or one that is to be done in the future. Thus the verse can be translated as

Become holy for holy am I, Hashem your God[3]

In this context we ask the question when is it that we do not recognize the presence of God in a situation? This occurs when something happens that we do not expect and/or do not want to happen, a situation which we interpret as devoid of the presence of God, thus a situation in which God is concealed.

However, there is only one force in the world and that is the force of God. Therefore, if we interpret a situation as devoid of God, in our consciousness, there is something else in the situation instead of God. Thus we experience deficiency, a deficiency of holiness.

What kind of inner work do we have to do to change a situation which we interpret as deficient in holiness to one which we interpret as full of holiness? Clearly we must change something in our consciousness. But what?

Here we must recognize that everything in our consciousness has a dimension of appearance and a dimension of essence. Furthermore, the same thing that has the dimension of essence at another level of conscious interpretation can have the dimension of appearance. Even, it is possible to hold multiple levels simultaneously. Whatever our interpretation or interpretations we hold, the choice is our choice. And that choice establishes our inner reality. We express this inner reality and impress it into the physical world which then reflects back to us our choice on the level of appearance.

---

[1]The usual translation of the unpronouncable eternal name would typically write the Lord. Here we write instead Hashem which is the Hebrew word that literally means the name.

[2]Leviticus 19:1-2

[3]Leviticus 19:1-2

Appearance is what is outer observed. Essence is what is inner grasped. Grasped means directly accepted and understood, without words or analysis. Anything analyzed becomes appearance in the analysis. What is inner grasped is deep, not analyzable, and carries mystery. For God is deep. His ways are not ways that can be fully understood. There is always a depth and mystery.

The Zohar tells us that when we come to the court of final judgment at the end of our days, we are going to be asked: What evil did you turn to good? Translated into the terms we have been using: What apparent deficiency of holiness in your consciousness did you change to full holiness in your consciousness. What inner work did you do to recognize essence in what you only saw as appearance?

The verse in Leviticus refers to this inner work. It is this inner work that we must do that is in the imperfect tense in Hebrew. It is that becoming that God is calling upon us to do: Become holy. Become holy by recognizing the essence, which is holy, behind the appearance. Do not live on automatic pilot. For every appearance, there is an essence. Grasp that essence and bring it into consciousness. This is the holiness we are called upon to fulfill.

In a modern language, this is the God consciousness toward which we are moving. Indeed, this is the God consciousness of the Era of Moshiach.

He who wants to experience the Holy
Must be dedicated to the Holy

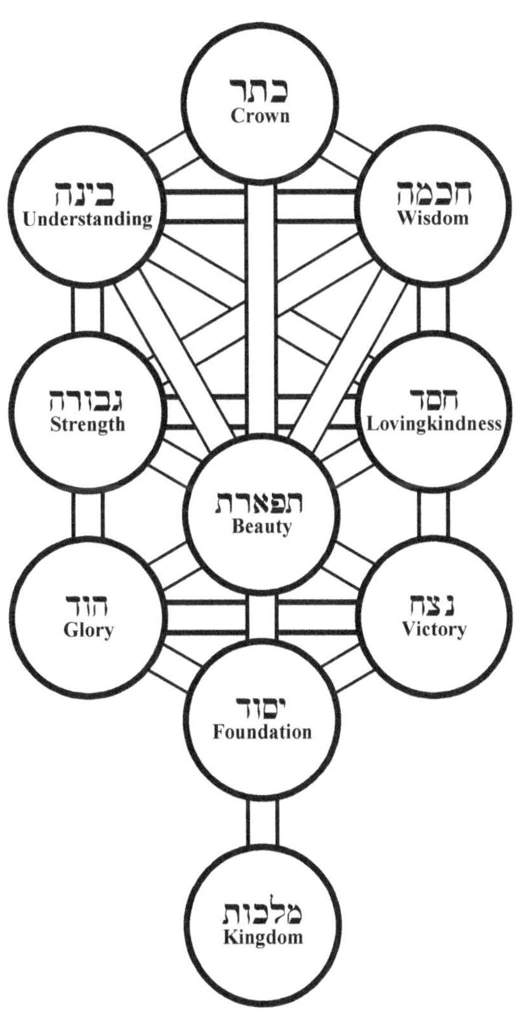

The Tree of Life

art_tree.ps

Consciousness of The Mystery

God is. God exists, but not in existence. Wherever we look, there is God. There is no place without the infiniteness of the Holy presence. The Oneness is amazing. It is awesome.

But if we see objectively, like an instrument, we will not get a hint of the Glory of God. What an instrument sees and measures is only appearance, limited and finite. We can only be conscious of essence[1] at a level of mystery, depth and unlimitedness.

Essence does not show up in a mechanical way. Awareness of Essence requires our consciousness to transcend appearance. This transcendence can occur when we will to hold the awareness of the mystery of God. This is a mystery whose depth is not penetrable. Its Oneness cannot be rationally and logically analyzed. It is a mystery that must be felt. It is not public. It is inner and private.

When we are conscious of the Mystery, we participate in the Oneness of God. We are able to simultaneously hold opposing or contradictory points of view without the necessity of resolving one over the other. Logical consistency and preference remain in suspended animation until we have to take an action which depends on which way we judge things.

There is a story told in the Tikkunei Zohar about a cripple and Torah scholars. Who the people in the story are are certainly not what they appear to be.

---

[1] essence here means ultimate essence

The Story

On the road the cripple meets a couple of Torah scholars who are on horseback. He greets them with greeting

> Shalom to the Leaders of the Generation.

They greet him. He asks them where they are going. He says he is going there too. If they like, he can arrange accommodations for them.

The Torah scholars are baffled. To arrange accommodations the cripple would have to arrive ahead of the them. But he is walking and a cripple and they are on horseback. They decide to indulge the cripple and accept his offer of accommodations. Then in a wink of an eye, the cripple runs and makes the road beneath his feet contract and before the Torah scholars have even gotten a chance to understand what happened, the cripple has disappeared. Then, immediately when the cripple arrives, he makes the road beneath the horses feet contract and he brings the Torah scholars to the destination.

The cripple, who is no cripple, leads the Torah scholars into the cave and takes a seat at his throne. Around him are 300 disciples all singing the beginning verse from Ecclesiastes.

> *Vanity of Vanities, Vanity of Vanities, all is Vanity.*

The Torah scholars do not know what to make of this. They ask the cripple,

> Do they know any other Torah verses to sing?

The cripple answers the question saying

> Do you not know that God created the universe with this verse?

Then he takes their hand and leads them to the first palace and on the door it is inscribed: *Vanity of Vanities, Vanity of Vanities, all is Vanity.*

Likewise at the second palace, the third, the fourth, the fifth, and the sixth. At the seventh palace the inscription reads the same with the addition

> Only those that know the meaning of this verse can enter here.

And as the cripple leads them to enter the palace, the Torah scholars, who are not Torah scholars, not knowing the meaning of the verse cannot enter. So the cripple makes the earth contract beneath their feet and returns them and their horses to the place in the road that they originally met.

Understanding the Story

To understand the story, we must understand the next verse of Ecclesiastes.

> *What profit does man have for all his labor which he toils beneath the sun?*

The sun is a metaphor for the rational intellect. The rational intellect deals with appearance. What profit does man have for all his intellectual labor, his logic, and his analysis, his technology, his science, his laws? Does it lead him to the glory of God? Does it lead him to God consciousness? Does it lead him to the Oneness of God? Certainly not if it is under the sun.

Everything that is experienced as only appearance is vanity, is futile. The only profit is to participate in the Oneness of God by letting the appearance point to the essence, which is necessarily experienced interior and private.

This means we must engage the world, work in it, manipulate the appearances. But we must do so with a consciousness that is beyond the appearances.

To labor with appearances, we must judge. Judgments are limiting because everything we judge becomes, for us, what we judged it to be. Essence cannot exist in a consciousness which judges what it considers essence to be.

Appearance can be defined. It can be named. And by naming it takes on the character of being limited and finite. Experience appearance without naming, and the experience becomes an experience of unlimited essence, unlimited oneness.

The Glory of God is concealed within the world of appearance. And it is this very appearance together with the appropriate state of our consciousness that can reveal the essence through the appearance. This is how we accomplish the unification of the letters Yod Hey Vav Hey יהוה of the unnameable and unpronounceable name of God. We hold the appearance with the essence together in unity. One is nameable, judgeable, and finite and the other is not nameable, not judgeable, and infinite.

Inner and Outer Reality

In first analysis, it appears that there is an outer reality external to us and an inner reality that is our aliveness. This is duality. Let us explore further.

The outer reality is appearance. It is only appearance. In Kabbalah, appearance is called *Klippah*, meaning husk or shell. Each instance of appearance must be given an interpretation. The interpretation governs the meaning and the significance the appearance has. The interpretation defines the essence of the appearance for the one who is conscious of it.

We have complete freedom as to how we define the essence of the appearance. For many people that choice is not a conscious choice. The first step in increasing God consciousness is to recognize that the choice of the interpretation we give to appearance is our own creation. If we desire God consciousness, then our interpretation must be related to the ultimate essence: God.

What does it consciously mean to relate to ultimate essence? It means to recognize that behind the appearance we encounter is the hand of God. This is God consciousness. This is wisdom.

God gives us limited time to live our inner reality. That we have any time at all is a gift. But it is deeper. If we had infinite time, then we would have no sense of the need to move toward God consciousness. We could indefinitely delay knowing there is yet time. Therefore, moving toward God consciousness itself would not have ultimate meaning.

Because our time is limited, moving toward God consciousness has ultimate meaning for us. To live fully, means that we must fill each moment with depth of meaning, depth of significance. Each moment must be lived as sacred. Each moment must be lived as holy. Each moment must have full passion for the living. Each moment must be completely authentic. Between us and others, there must be a harmonious interchange. Those close to us must be loved completely, with care, respect and reverence.

The center of God consciousness is love. For love gives essence to the one being loved. When the one we love wants to play, we want to play. When the one we love wants to be with us with joy, we are with them with joy. When the one we love needs help, we immediately help. When the one we love needs comfort, we immediately provide comfort. When the one we love needs attention, we immediately provide attention. We do everything we can to help make the one we love be happy. In this way we become the complete lover to our beloved.

If we become conscious of something negative in our beloved, we become conscious of something that is appearance. For essence is not negative. The degree that we maintain this consciousness and do not transcend it, is the degree to which our love becomes limited. And this is the degree to which we are no longer the complete lover of our beloved.

What is true in the relationship between humans as lover and beloved, is true in our relationship between humans and God. Where we have a consciousness of negativity, a lack of fullness in our situation, our consciousness has moved to toward living appearance alone. Living appearance alone is to live deficiency. Deficiency moves us away from God. When we let go of deficiency and limitation, we engage in the full splendor of living God.

The center of God consciousness is love. We must completely love those closest to us. Anything less means that the moment we live is not fully endowed with essence. We must completely love God. Anything less means that the moment we live and the situation in which we live is not fully endowed with essence. In this sense, each moment and situation must not be limited. If it is not fully endowed with essence, our God consciousness will be limited. If our God consciousness is limited, our living is limited. We will not have full freedom for creative sacred living.

The degree to which our God consciousness is limited, is the degree to which we are conscious of and relate to appearances without essence. When this happens, we either choose to repulse the appearance and live it deficiently, becoming negatively attached to it. Or we become indifferent to it. Or we desire it and become positively attached to it. If we become indifferent to it, there is no relation and hence no essence. In either the case of repulsion or the case of desire, our own ego grows with the strength of the attachment. We chain ourselves and become slaves to it.

Why do we become slaves when we attach either positively or negatively to appearance? Because in the end, the attachment is not ultimately satisfying. In negative attachment we become occupied with destroying the appearance. And we become dissatisfied. In positive attachment, we want more of it. No matter how much we have, we want more of it. And if we cannot get more, then we become dissatisfied. In either case, this dissatisfaction is a dis-satiation. We live a deficiency. When we live a deficiency we suffer.

The Eastern approach stresses living mindfully with detachment. For the attachment leads to suffering. Suffering disrupts internal peace and bliss. The Western approach stresses filling our consciousness of God, so that everything is meaningful. It is less important whether or not something is a hardship for us. It is more important whether or not it is meaningful for us and whether or not that meaning relates to Godliness.

In a certain sense, the Eastern approach and the Western approach are two sides of the same coin. Each has its place. And to do one completely means, in essence, to do the other completely. A person who understands this will be able to use both disciplines to move more effectively to greater God consciousness: the one discipline being to consciously give essence to each appearance, thereby transcending the limitation of the appearance; the other discipline being to detach oneself from the consciousness of appearance alone so that there is the room in consciousness for ultimate essence, God.

It is a rule of reality that internally, either essence or appearance is lived.[1] Where there is consciousness of appearance, there is no essence. Where there is essence, there is no consciousness of appearance. For with appearance is ego; where there is ego there cannot be God.

Our condition is that with each new situation, if we are not mindful enough, we bring appearance into our internal reality. Our job then becomes one of transcending the appearance, alone. We transcend the appearance, by giving such a full essence to it, that we live the essence and not the appearance. When we are successful in doing that, ego becomes minimized, even nullified. In Kabbalah, we say that we draw down the Divine light. And although we draw down the Divine light, we stay simply humble. Dis-satisfaction disappears. Suffering is no more. In its place is bliss, an internal quietness, a satisfying peace, a holiness, a closeness to God.

When we consistently live this kind of closeness to God, the duality and separateness of appearance and essence begins to fade away. For the place of appearance is the hiddenness of God. The hiddenness of God is that dimension of God's transcendence to which we can relate.

As transcendence means going beyond, God's transcendence must of necessity be hidden. Although we do not experience the revelation of His transcendence, we can experience that it is there in its hidden aspect, the first aspect we can be conscious of. Then when we transcend appearance, we parallel in our individual way, God's transcendence. In this way, we mirror the Divine. This is what it means to run and return.

Living in this way, we become aware of an unconditional unity. Here consciousness becomes the place where the unity of God is revealed. This unity is the Divine light of the Oneness of God.

Now we are ready to understand some verses in Deuteronomy.

> *Listen Isreal! Hashem is our God, Hashem is One.*
>
> *You shall love Hashem, your God, with all your heart, with all your soul and with all your resources (your everything). And these matters that I command you today shall be upon your heart.*

---

[1] We can be conscious of both essence and appearance. But we make a choice of one and in the moment live with only that choice.

You shall teach them thoroughly to your children.

And you shall speak of them during the times when you are sitting in your home, when you are walking on the way, when you are lying down, and when you are rising up.

Bind them as a sign upon your arm and let them be ornaments between your eyes. And write them on the doorposts of your house and upon your gates.[2]

The verses start with the proclamation of the unity of God. *Listen Israel!* Listen all you spiritual seekers. *Hashem*, who we understand as God Transcendent, *is our God*, the God that we personally experience, the God that is Immanent. *Hashem is one.* God Immanent and God Transcendent are one.

God transcendant, who manifests in this world as hidden within the appearance is identically the same as the God immanent, God who reveals Himself in and through all His creation.

The verses then continue, giving us the prescription for our own conscious realization and living experience of this.

You shall love Hashem, your God, with all your heart, with all your soul and with all your resources.

This is the complete love of God we have already discussed. All our heart, meaning all our desires. All our soul, meaning all our spirit. All our resources, meaning all our everything, even beyond the everything we currently have.

If we are as lover to God, then we respond to Him as a lover responds to the beloved. He wants to be with us in joy and fullness. So we are with Him in joy and fullness. Although God is not deficient in any way and needs nothing from us, nevertheless He tells us what He wants from us. He wants us to live in a particular way. That way is the commandments, the law of God. And because we are His lover, and He wants us to live in accordance with the law, in accordance with Torah. We live our love to Him by living in accordance with his commandments.

You shall teach them thoroughly to your children.

And it is these commandments and the way of Torah, God's ways, that He wants us to teach to our children so that our children may know and experience God, the way we know and experience God, the way God wants us to know and experience Him.

[2]Deuteronomy 6:4-9

> *And you shall speak of them during the times when you are sitting in your home, when you are walking on the way, when you are lying down, and when you are rising up.*
>
> *Bind them as a sign upon your arm and let them be ornaments between your eyes. And write them on the doorposts of your house and upon your gates.*

Now consider all the activities in which we are daily involved. We speak to others. We sit and be with them. We walk and travel with them. We lie down and get up with them. We do work with our hands. We perceive with our eyes. We move from one entranceway to another.

All these are ordinary everyday activities. These situations are given to us in their appearance. But the appearance is the hiddenness of God. It is the husk or shell. The husk is the dry external covering of certain fruits or seeds. In general it is the outer part of anything, especially when the outer part is worthless by itself.

But it is the outer part that preserves and protects the inner part, the essence. Listen to what these verses are telling us.

> You first see the outer part, the appearance. Remember that the outer part is worthless. It is only the carrier of the Divine essence. If you want to experience Me, to the extent possible in this physical world, then you must parallel My transcendence. In love for Me, you must transcend the appearance. You must regard the appearance as a sacred and unique entranceway, an entranceway in time that I have especially created for you. This entranceway, is the entranceway that can make the lived moment eternal.
>
> Transcending does not mean finding the inherent essence of the appearance as if the inherent essence is independent of your consciousness. You are a living being. I created you in My image. The meaning of the appearance is governed by your consciousness. You are free to choose it as you like. You are free to be conscious of it as you like. This is your freedom, freedom that I give as a gift to you.
>
> You can be conscious of the appearance as appearance. You can give an ordinary culturally acceptable meaning to the appearance. You can be conscious of it only as mechanical cause and effect or only in terms of the cultural values of your society. Or, you can express your love to Me by transcending the appearance.
>
> Listen to Me. Go through the entranceway of each moment, for it is a beginning to eternity, by being conscious of essence and not

the appearance. Give that appearance the meaning of the essence of My Divine Kingship. Make the appearance holy and sacred to you. This is how you will have God consciousness. This is how you will be conscious of my Kingship. This is how you can make your world My dwelling place. This is my Oneness. This is how you must love Me.

Garment

Rabbi Voloshin, in quoting the Zohar says:

> Everything, above or below, beginning with the mystery of the Upper Point down to the last of the degrees of creation, is arranged thus: everything is a garment for something else, and that which is concealed by a garment, is in turn a garment for another ... one within the other ... until the first is a husk for the second, and the second is a husk for the third, and so on.

Similarly in the *Idra Zutra:*

> And all lights are united in one; this light shines in that one, and that one in this. ... The light which is revealed is called the garment of the King, and the very inner light, is that known as the Hidden Light.

Appearance and Essence

0

Appearance is in unity.
Essence is in unity.

1

Essence is full.
Appearance is empty.

2

Everything has its appearance.
But its appearance is not its essence.

Everything has its essence.
But its essence is not its appearance.

3

Appearance is the manifestation of essence.
Essence is an idealization of appearance.

Appearance is instance.
Essence is meaning.

Appearance is thing or action.
Essence is symbol and relation.

4

Appearance conceals the essence.
Essence reveals through appearance.

Appearance gives existence to essence.
Essence gives unity to appearance.

Appearance is somewhere.
And being somewhere is separated.

Essence is nowhere.
And being nowhere is everywhere.

5

Appearance is garment.
Essence is body.

Appearance is body.
Essence is heart.

Appearance is heart.
Essence is mind.

Appearance is mind.
Essence is soul.

Appearance is soul.
Essence is God.

6

Appearance is in physical existence.
Essence is beyond physical existence.

Appearance has form.
Essence is formless.

Appearance has boundary.
Essence is without boundary.

Appearance has place.
Essence has no place.

Appearance is temporal.
Essence is eternal.

Appearance is in motion.
Essence is motionless.

7

Appearance is seen.
Essence is unseen.

Appearance is heard.
Essence is silent.

Appearance can be touched.
Essence is untouchable.

Appearance can be tasted.
Essence is not tastable.

Appearance can be smelled.
Essence is not smellable.

Appearance can be thought.
Essence is not thinkable.

Appearance is divided.
Essence is not dividable.

8

Appearance is transitory and changeable.
Essence is permanent and changeless.

Appearance is outer observed.
Essence is inner grasped.

Appearance is compound.
Essence is simple.

Appearance is descended essence.
Essence is ascended appearance.

Appearance is what receives.
Essence is what gives.

Appearance is physical.
Essence is spiritual.

Appearance is named.
Essence is unnamed.

Appearance is finite.
Essence is infinite.

9

Appearance is the Many.
Essence is the One.

Introduction To The Commentary

When consciousness meets reality, reality does not imprint itself in consciousness. For sure consciousness has the awareness of what can be called the phenomena, the data our senses give to us about reality. But we pay little attention to our sense data on a purely descriptive level. Rather, our consciousness interprets that descriptive sense data. The interpretation has two components: Appearance and Essence.

Appearance and Essence arise in consciousness and do not independently exist in the reality outside of us. Often one, Appearance, is in conscious awareness and the other, Essence, is in our subconscious.

The subconscious is useful as it helps us run on autopilot while we direct our conscious focus on something else. However, as our subconscious autopilot can be exerting some control over us, it can limit and bind us. The only way to break out of the binding is elevate both Appearance and Essence to conscious awareness where our faculties of desire, reason, intuition and will can act in concert to make us transcend our momentary limitation.

How do desire, reason, intuition, and will act in concert? By recognizing that Appearance and Essence arise out of our interpretation, an interpretation that is not given as being part of the reality outside of us. When we recognize that our interpretation is internal, and not part of the independently existing reality outside of ourselves, we can discover that there are usually multiple consistent interpretations. We usually prefer one and are not aware that there could be others. Our consciousness impresses into reality the interpretations we choose. Then we become responsible for the choice we made.

The first step in an expanded consciousness is to recognize that there are multiple interpretations and be able to simultaneously hold in consciousness even multiple possibly contradictory interpretations. Holding in consciousness here means playing with and experiencing the different interpretations. Playing with them gives us time to avoid mistakes. We are able to suspend externalizing quick judgments in order to settle on that interpretation by which the hand of the Divine becomes most present to us. This is the interpretation that we wish to imprint into and make part of the reality in which we live.

Appearance and Essence explains how to do this.

First Commentary

0

The beginning is a division of consciousness into that which consciousness understands as Appearance and that which consciousness understands as Essence. But both are in unity.

How can there be a division when both are in the same unity? If they are in the same unity then, they must be the same. But how can they be the same if they are called by different names?

1

These verses assert that Essence is full and Appearance is empty. If they were just different terms for the same thing then one could not be full and the other empty. So we understand that they cannot be the same.

2

Further supporting this assertion that Appearance and Essence are not the same, we learn that everything in consciousness has its Appearance and has its Essence, but the one is not the other.

3

Here we learn that the two aspects of consciousness being described are related. Essence can only manifest through Appearance, but the Appearance is not the Essence. The Appearance, however, is the clothing of the Essence, its shell, or as the kabbalists would say, its Klippah. As Appearance is the manifestation of Essence, Essence is the idealization of Appearance.

If we choose, we can deal with Appearance alone as if it is the only aspect of the reality our consciousness may be aware. In this case, Appearance is instance, thing, or action and no more. It is the backside which can be seen. Essence is the front side and is the meaning we give to the Appearance. Meaning is in the world of symbol, value, and relation.

4

Essence cannot be directly seen, but is revealed through the Appearance clothing it. But this revealment is not direct. For the Appearance itself conceals the Essence. How can that which reveals be that which conceals? So here we learn that we cannot think of the reality we live as that which is outside of us. In each and every moment, we make a choice as to how to consciously frame what we see, hear, smell, taste, and touch. Depending on how we consciously frame it, our experience is an encounter with Appearance or an encounter with unity of Essence and Appearance. And this is the meaning of Appearance gives existence to Essence, for that which is not in our consciousness, has no existence for us.

Living in a conscious reality of Appearances, we encounter everything as being separate, located in places separated from one another. But Essence has no place. Nowhere can it be experienced as Appearance. Yet when consciousness frames the Essence of our encounter, we experience unity, everywhere we look.

5

Here we learn that there are levels. On the one hand we are conscious of Appearance as garment, then our encounter with Essence will be the body. If we are conscious of Appearance as body, then our encounter with Essence will be as heart. If we are conscious of Appearance as heart, then our encounter with Essence will be as mind. If we are conscious of Appearance as mind, then our encounter with Essence will be as soul. If we are conscious of Appearance as soul, then our encounter with Essence will be a connection to God.

It is we who chose what level our consciousness is on. Whatever level it is on, Essence is on the next level, just beyond where our rational consciousness has settled. So we see that on any level, Appearance and Essence are the backside and front side of our encounter on that level.

But our consciousness does not have to be on only one level. We can choose to live our encounter on multiple levels simultaneously. And the more levels we live our encounters, the greater unity we will experience.

6

To be clear about Appearance, Appearance is in what consciousness interprets as physical reality. Essence, is beyond physical reality. Thus, everything in physical reality has form, but that which is beyond physical reality has no form. Everything in physical reality has boundary, but that which is beyond physical reality has no boundary. Everything in physical reality has place, but that which is beyond physical reality has no place. Everything in physical reality is temporal. But that which is beyond physical reality is eternal. Everything in physical reality is in motion, but that which is beyond physical reality has no motion.

7

To further clarify Appearance, Appearance is what is measurable through sight, hearing, touch, taste and smell. If we were to try to measure essence, the essence would disappear and become Appearance. To be conscious of Essence means we have to hold in consciousness that which is not measurable and that which is not dividable. We have to hold in consciousness the Oneness.

8

Now it becomes clear that Appearance is what is externalizable, or outer observed. Essence is inner, not inner observable for that which is observable is Appearance, but inner grasped. Not grasped like the linear flow of a logical argument, but grasped at the level of the flash of intuition, before we process the intuition and verbalize it into a thought stream of words. So at whatever level or levels we are consciously holding, Essence is beyond words. Essence can only be held as the deep mystery of the oneness we can choose to encounter. It is held as simple, permanent, changeless, spiritual, unnamed, and infinite.

9

In the end, we understand Appearance to be the diverse manyfold aspect of the reality we consciously live and essence as the Oneness beyond that reality. In the end, Essence is God in whom we rejoice. Essence is the reality beyond reality that we can sense. Essence is a reality in whose creation we have to participate.

Second Commentary

The first commentary does not directly answer the initial question. How can Appearance and Essence both be in the same unity?

The problem is with the question. For it supposes that Appearance and Essence are things. Things are separated and cannot exist in the same space. But Appearance and Essence are not things. Appearance is what our senses bring to consciousness. It is in the world of our consciousness. The issue is what we do with what comes to our consciousness. What we do is unify it with a meaning, its ultimate Essence. If we choose that Essence to be only the plain immediate common sense meaning, we live and experience that level of Essence. If we choose that Essence to be beyond the plain immediate common sense meaning, we live and experience that beyond level of Essence.

The verse Appearance is in unity; Essence is in unity is written from the perspective of the spiritual seeker whose work is to unify the physical reality held in consciousness with the presence of God. For the spiritual seeker, Appearance is in unity; and Essence is in unity. The unity is the unification of Appearance with Essence. This unification is exactly the unification of the letters of great eternal name of Hashem, the unification of the Yod-Hey יה with the Vav-Hey וה as is written in the traditional prayer books.

The Appearance given to us, is given by God. The Essence we unify the Appearance with is what we give back to God. And by the Essence we choose to make the unification, we change the Appearance. Therefore, from our perspective Essence gives and Appearance receives. From God's perspective, Appearance is given and Essence is received.

The Essence which is most beyond, is not objectifiable and not analyzable. That Essence is presence of God.

From this point of view we can understand the meaning of the passage when Moses says to God:

> *Show me now Your glory.*[1]

God replies

> *I shall make all My goodness pass before you and I shall call out with the Name Hashem before you; I shall show graciousness when I choose to show graciousness, and I shall show mercy when I choose to show mercy.*[2]

---

[1]Exodus 33:18
[2]Exodus 33:19

And God continues

> *You will not be able to see My face, for no human can see My face and live. Behold, there is a place near Me; you may stand on the rock. When My glory passes by, I shall place you in a cleft of the rock; I shall shield you with My hand until I have passed, Then I shall remove My hand and you will see My back, but My face may not be seen.*[3]

Moses is asking to see Essence. But Moses' request is not just his request of thousands of years ago. It is the request of each spiritual seeker. God replies that His goodness continuously passes by us. Indeed it passes by as Appearance. But we will not be able to see God's face, for seeing God's face would mean seeing Essence. But Essence cannot be seen. God tells Moses

> *You will see My back, but My face may not be seen.*

Back here means Appearance. What consciousness can receive is only the back of God. This is the goodness that God gives us. We cannot receive or comprehend God's essence or comprehend how God gives existence. This is beyond us. What we can receive is the Appearance that our senses give to our consciousness.

Our unification of that Appearance with Essence defines how we experience God in our world. That unification depends on our interpretation. Thus there are levels. At the lowest level, our unification creates an idol which we hold in consciousness. To the degree to which we create an idol, our consciousness cannot hold the mystery of God. At the highest level our unification, we are God conscious; our consciousness holds the mystery of God together with the Appearance that God gives us. And this is the meaning of

> *Taste and see that he Lord is good. Happy is the man who seeks refuge in Him.*[4]

---

[3]Exodus 33:20-23

[4]Psalms 34:9

Third Commentary

Five year old Shirley is walking through the field to visit her aunt Poly. On the way she picks some wild flowers to give to Poly. As she walks into Poly's house with her wild flowers, Poly screams: "What are you doing bring dirty soil into my house with these flowers?"

For Poly, the appearance is the flowers but the essence is the dirty soil clinging to the roots of the plants Shirley is bringing into the house.

For Shirley, the dirt does not even exist. The appearance is the flowers and the essence is her love that she is bringing to her aunt. The flowers are a token of her love.

On another level, the appearance is the love and the essence is that aspect of God that she recognizes in her aunt.

The conflict is all about what is in each person's consciousness relative to appearance and essence. When there is agreement, there is harmony and peace. Worlds blossom. When there is difference, there is anger and upheaval. Worlds clash.

Unifying

When in our consciousness the One becomes many, its oneness becomes hidden in the many. We sense that the Divine presence retreats to our secret place and becomes veiled. When in our consciousness the many becomes the one, the Divine presence becomes manifest.

There is nothing that can stop the expression of the spirit, Whatever it is that we do, the result is an expression of our spirit, our soul. What we do does make a difference, for the expression can be unifying in which case, it is called good. Or the expression can be separating, in which case it is called bad.

The Divine urges us to express unification and not separation. The individual who expresses unification acts to close the circuit, letting the spirit grasp and surround and envelope the form which grows out of itself. But the individual who expresses separation acts to break the circuit removing the spirit from the form. And since the form cannot sustain itself without the spirit, the form itself must break down into its more elementary components permitting the spirit to reform the physical into a new individual.

When we experience this breaking down, we go through tough times. We suffer. But it is the reforming, which is our transcending, that brings us to a new higher level of formation. This permits even deeper and more complex expressions of our Godly soul which desires to express unification.

Connection

When my state is one of connection,
The appearance I see,
Is connected to its essence,
And are married together by my primal intent,
To receive for the sake of sharing.
All is in unity.

When my state is one of separateness,
The appearances I see,
Are separated from their essence,
And are divorced by my primal intent,
To receive for myself alone.
Ten thousand things are in strife.

Essence Responds To Essence

In playing an infinite game, the infinite player expresses freedom. The real meaning of freedom is that of essence responding to essence, our essence responding to Godly essence. What can an essence response be? To understand this we must first understand what could be the essence that the Divine is expressing.

Russell says:

> The perpetuity of Creation is based upon the constant giving of one half of a cycle to the other half for the purpose of repeating the creative process through another cycle of giving for regiving.[1]

What is being given is a sharing of Divine Oneness. Now Oneness cannot be comprehended without its opposite, multiplicity. And the Oneness which is shared is a Oneness which changes to the appearance of multiplicity which we by our understanding come to experience as the Oneness from which it came. Thus, Oneness is not a static experience. It is a dynamic becoming in which we play an integral part.

To explain this idea of Oneness and multiplicity, Russell considers the ocean.

> Its unchanging stillness, unbroken by waves of motion which seemingly divide it into many measurable units, might be likened to the stillness of the one Light of God's unchanging knowing, broken by the thinking of that knowing into many seemingly changing and measurable parts. Upon that calm ocean there are no separate or separable units to give multiplicity or individuality to its oneness. There is nothing there which changes, nothing to measure. One could not put his finger anywhere upon it and return to locate that same point, for every point upon it anywhere is the same point. There is no everywhere in it, for there is not extension in it - nothing that is relative to any other thing - for there is no other thing in the ocean's oneness for it to be relative to....
>
> The moment the still balance of the ocean becomes extended to two unbalanced opposite conditions, the unchanging oneness becomes a changing multiplicity. The unity of the ocean idea is divided into wave units of that idea. Separateness and separability come into seeming being when one can count oneness into infinity - where

[1] Walter Russell, *The Message of the Divine Iliad*, University of Science and Philosophy, Waynesboro, VA, 22980, p88

> the measureless can be measured - where variation from oneness gives individuality to varying and changing units.
>
> Wherever unity is manifested by infinite numbers of units no two of those units are alike. Likewise, where one balanced equal pressure is divided into two opposite unbalanced pressures, motion becomes imperative for the purpose of seeking balance.
>
> The import of this is the fact that all divisibility and multiplicity, all individuality, changing, measure, unbalance and disunity come from Oneness - from the Transcendent Unity itself. All of these qualities of separateness return to the oneness from which they came for the purpose of again expressing their separateness in infinite numbers of forever changing multiplicities.
>
> That fact of the division and multiplication of unity of God's *knowing* into the infinity of God's *thinking* - for taking His One Idea apart and expressing it as many parts - then putting all those parts together again into the unity from which they came - is the one dominant characteristic of Creation. That is what Creation is - many changing units of moving light waves arising from the stillness of the one light; then returning to that stillness for rebirth into light waves of motion....
>
> In this manner life springs from oneness to manifest one half of the life cycle, and returns to oneness as death to manifest the other half. This is the inviolate order of Nature. There is no other order. That is the law of Nature. There is no other law than that one of rhythmic balanced interchange between the opposite halves of cycles which forever spring from oneness to manifest oneness in multiple forms of individual expressions. [2]

God is always sharing Divine Beneficence: "balanced interchange between opposite halves of cycles which forever spring from oneness to manifest oneness in multiple forms of individual expressions." This is the light. This is the essence. The essence of our response is an acknowledgment of receiving Divine Beneficence and our sharing of this Beneficence in our human world. So we bless and we do. The blessing is our internal ceremony of acknowledgment that we have received Divine Beneficence. Such blessings we can also make external if we wish. In the world of appearance, the doing is our actions by which things that appear to be in opposition can be harmonized. The essence of this

[2] ibid, pp .93-96

appearance is the beneficence which we share by this doing. And this doing not only causes change, but is an integral part of Change.

> Oneness is not material. The cycle begins with God's Transcendent Oneness, With God giving his Oneness to us, In appearance, in manyfoldness. We receive the manyfoldness and By linking the manyfoldness to God, We transform the manyfoldness to the Transcendent Oneness, Which we return to God.

God, The Tetragrammaton, The Infinite Game, Change

The Tetragrammaton is the unpronounceable name of God, יהוה. The four letters stand for the four worlds: the world of emanation, the world of creation, the world of formation, and the world of manifestation. Think for a moment what these four worlds mean. The world of emanation is the spiritual world of archetype concepts. The world of creation is the world in which the archetype concept is particularized. The world of formation is the plan whereby the physical creation of the archetype concept can come into existence. The plan is the plan of action. The world of manifestation is the world in which the action takes place, following the plan, to bring into physical existence the new creation.

The thought of the Divine comes through these four worlds. Physical existence is just the carrier, the medium, by which the thought gets expressed. So physical existence is just the appearance. The thought, itself, is the essence. The essence is never the carrier, which is only the appearance.

Zalman writes:

> The meaning of the Tetragrammaton is "that which calls everything into being" (מהוה את הכל. Now מהוה is the simple present tense. The letter Yod (י) is substituted for the letter Mem (מ) giving the name יהוה. The prefix Yod (י) added to the stem הוה indicates not only a present, but a continuous action as Rashi remarks in his comment to the verse: "In this manner used Job to do all the days" (Job I 5). The Tetragrammaton, then, represents the Life which flows down actually *at every moment* unto all creatures and calls them forth at each moment out of nothingness.[1]

The result of the Divine thought is something which comes into physical existence. We perceive this coming into physical existence as a becoming or as a changing. Something happens which was not there before. Something is different.

Our world, therefore, is a changing world. The world is not constant. We are part of this changing world. We encounter change. We change. We initiate change. And we have to adapt to the change initiated by others. Adapting means that we too have to change in ways that we did not anticipate. Our world is a

---

[1] Shneur Zalman, *The Portal of Unity and Faith* in Raphael Ben Zion, *An Anthology of Jewish Mysticism*, The Judaica Press, Inc. New York, 1981, p95-96.

world of surprises: surprises that are given to us and surprises that we give to others.

These surprises come when our comfortable state of being has become completed in time. This means that just when we are comfortable, then we find there is Change. But within us, our ego likes security. Security means constancy. And constancy is not in the world of manifestation. At the physical level, this beingness is in the becoming.

Becoming means that the freedom that we have must be utilized to initiate change and to adapt to change. This adaptation manifests in the physical world. But this is only its appearance. The essence of this becoming is in the higher worlds.

The cycle can be easily described. Godly essence gives rise to changing appearance, which is a carrier for the expression of the essence. We respond to changing appearance by our becoming: changing our thoughts, words, and actions. This response is our expression of an essence. The response itself is also carried by a changing appearance. But the appearance is not the essence for us either. This essence which is expressed through the changing appearance of our becoming, returns back to God.

To emphasize this point of view, we will discuss change in its essence, which we denote by Change. There are two ways in which we can participate in Change: by playing a finite game or by playing an infinite game. When we play a finite game we are finite players. When we play an infinite game, we are infinite players.

To encourage Change is to participate in it. To encourage Change in oneself is to play an infinite game. To participate in Change is to be surprised. To be surprised is to move boundaries, remove limitations and experience the unexpected.

This means that

> Because infinite players prepare themselves to be surprised by the future, they play in complete openness. It is not an openness as in *candor*, but an openness as in *vulnerability*. It is not a matter of exposing one's unchanging identity, the true self that has always been, but a way of exposing one's ceaseless growth, the dynamic self that has yet to be. The infinite player does not expect only to be amused by surprise, but to be transformed by it.[2]

The infinite player plays for the essence, which is never to play in order to accomplish something. The infinite player plays in order that the game be

[2]James Carse, *Finite and Infinite Games*, Ballantine Books, New York, 1986, p23.

infinitely continued, that the game never end. Therefore, the rules change in the course of the game. In contrast, the finite player plays to accomplish something that he might be declared the winner and the game be ended. Therefore, the rules of the game do not change and because they do not change, the game has been internally limited. That is why it is called a finite game.

When the infinite player moves boundaries and experiences surprise the infinite player discovers that

> the infinite play of life is joyous. Infinite play resounds throughout with a kind of laughter. It is not a laughter at others who have come to an unexpected end, having thought they were going somewhere else. It is laughter with others with whom we have discovered that the end we thought we were coming to has unexpectedly opened. We laugh not at what has surprisingly come to be impossible for others, but over what has surprisingly come to be possible with others. [3]

To suppress Change in oneself is to play a finite game. Though the finite player suppresses Change in himself, the finite player plays to surprise the opponent. For when the opponent has been sufficiently surprised, the finite game ends and the surpriser is declared the winner.

This means that

> Finite players must appear to be something other than what they are. Everything about their appearance must be concealing. To appear is not to appear. All the moves of a finite player must be deceptive; feints, distractions, falsifications, misdirections, mystifications. [4]

Not only do finite players not appear to be what they are, but they exist in contradiction. This is because for the finite player, the purpose of the game was to have accomplished something. Hence, life

> is not play, but the outcome of play. Finite players play to live; they do not live their playing. Life is therefore deserved, bestowed, possessed, won. It is not lived. [5]

The purpose of the finite play is to win. If one wins, one has won a title. There is no surprise and the game is over. So, the finite player after winning has not yet lived. If one loses, one has lost a title. There is no surprise and the game

[3] ibid, p31.

[4] ibid. p22.

[5] ibid. pp28-29.

is over. So, the finite player after losing has not yet lived. To win or lose a finite game is not to live because the purpose of the game was only to win or lose a title. A title is a statement of what one is. It is a statement of a static Being, not a statement about a dynamic Becoming. Carse explains:

> Because the purpose of a finite game is to bring play to an end with the victory of one of the players, each finite game is played to end itself. The contradiction is precisely that all finite play is play against itself.[6]

Play against play is serious. There can be no room to experience surprise in the play. There can be no room for uncertainty. There can be no room to remove limitations or remove boundaries. There can be no room for an open outcome. There can be no room for living.

In playing an infinite game, the infinite player expresses freedom. The real meaning of freedom is that of essence responding to essence, our essence responding to Godly essence. What can an essence response be? To understand this we must first understand what could be the essence which the Creation which the Divine is expressing.

Russell says:

> The perpetuity of Creation is based upon the constant giving of one half of a cycle to the other half for the purpose of repeating the creative process through another cycle of giving for regiving.[7]

What is being given is a sharing of Divine Oneness. Now Oneness cannot be comprehended without its opposite, multiplicity. And the Oneness which is shared is a Oneness which changes to the appearance of multiplicity which we by our understanding come to experience as the Oneness from which it came. Thus, Oneness is not a static experience. It is a dynamic becoming in which we play an integral part.

God is always sharing Divine Beneficence: "balanced interchange between opposite halves of cycles which forever spring from oneness to manifest oneness in multiple forms of individual expressions." This is the light. This is the essence. The essence of our response is an acknowledgement of receiving Divine Beneficence and our sharing of this Beneficence in our human world. So we bless and we do. The blessing is our internal ceremony of acknowledgement that we are have received Divine Beneficence. Such blessings we can also

---

[6]ibid, p29.

[7]Walter Russell, *The Message of the Divine Iliad*, University of Science and Philosophy, Waynesboro, VA, 22980, p88.

make external if we wish. In the world of appearance, the doing is our actions by which things that appear to be in opposition can be harmonized. The essence of this appearance is the beneficence which we share by this doing. And this doing not only causes change, but is an integral part of Change, Lee's word for God.

Lee says

> The Change is the beginning and the end of all process. Everything is in a process of becoming because of the Change. The Change is in everything, but everything is not the Change. The Change is both hidden in the depth of all things and manifest in the concrete process of becoming. The Change is not known by itself but by its manifestation only. It is manifest in everything, because everything owes its existence to the Change.
>
> Day changes to night and night to day because of the Change. Brightness changes to darkness and dark to bright because of the Change. Spring changes to summer and summer to autumn because of the Change. Coldness becomes warmth and warmth becomes coldness because of the Change. The Change makes trees grow and decay. Man is born and dies because he is part of the Change. The way of our thinking changes, the manner of our behavior changes, the system of our values changes, for the Change is active in all things. The strong becomes weak and the weak becomes strong because of the Change. The future becomes the present and the present becomes the past because of the Change. The Change makes the small great and the great small. Energy changes to mass and mass to energy, for they are relative to the power of the Change. Everything is in the process of change because of the Change. In the process of becoming changing can be gradual or rapid, for everything has its own trend in the changing process. The process of change is total and universal, for the Change is the inner essence of all existence.
>
> The Change is the mother of everything that exists in the universe. Being is possible because of becoming, and becoming is possible because of the Change. Being is not real by itself, but is real only in the process of becoming. Being itself is nothing but the illusion of becoming. Being is our misunderstanding of becoming. Being is our mental particularization of becoming, while becoming is the wholeness of being realized in the process of change. It is not the being which makes becoming possible, but the the becoming which makes being real. Being is totally dependent on becoming, for it is

> always relative to the Change. Becoming is not dependent on being but is meaningful because of being. Becoming is the realization of the Change, while being is the realization of becoming. Thus, without the Change becoming is not possible, and without becoming being is an illusion. The Change is the source of all creative process, because it has creativity within itself. The process of creativity through production and reproduction is possible because of the Change. Whenever there is growth and decay or expansion and contraction, there must be the Change. The Change is the moving mover of all the changes in the process of becoming.[8]

The internal manifestation of the Change is desire. Desire causes activity. Activity causes external change. Spontaneously experiencing this activity and the result of this activity is living. In living, we change internally. The internal change we make in ourselves causes new desires. Thus having begun in Change-caused desire, we return in desire-caused Change.

Living continues the creation. Without creation, nothing would change and there would be no movement. Change is Creation and man is an agent of Change.

Man's attempt to stop the realization of Change is man's attempt to put something permanent in place. This is a finite game. This is a game of restriction. This is a game of attempting to make something *be* rather than *become*, put the world in a state of being rather than its state of becoming. All such attempts in the end must fail for the nature of Change is to induce becoming, not being.

When our freedom of becoming is fully utilized, essence responds to essence and we experience fulfillment. When our freedom of becoming is not fully utilized we do not experience fulfillment. We experience unfulfillment. Unfulfillment is anxiety. Lee writes:

> Anxiety is freedom unrealized. When freedom is not fully realized anxiety arises. Freedom is based on the harmony of opposites, but anxiety is produced by the unfulfilled harmony. Anxiety is then based on the confusion of roles between the opposites.[9]

And what are these opposites? Opposites are anything which stand in opposition to one another. The prototype of opposites is the right and left columns of the tree of life: the water and the fire, the masculine and the feminine, the Yang and the Yin.

Lee explains:

---

[8]Jung Young Lee, *Cosmic Religion*, Philosophical Library Inc., New York, 1973, pp15-20.

[9]ibid, p61.

> Since everything has the interplay of Yin and Yang, the possibility of anxiety is inherent in all things. When the roles of Yin and Yang are confused, anxiety is produced. Yin is to be Yin and Yang is to be Yang in their relationship. They are not to be altered in a harmonious relationship. When their function is ambiguous, disruption arises. This disruption manifests itself as a form of anxiety.[10]

Harmony is the balancing of opposites, the balancing of Yin and Yang. Balancing requires opposites. The creation of harmony is not accomplished in attempting to annihilate or alter the natures of Yin and Yang. It is in the juxtaposing them in the right positions so that they naturally balance one another.

An important point which is raised here is that whatever we do to bring the opposites into harmony, we only create new more interesting possibilities for opposites to be out of harmony. This may sound like a hopeless situation. But put this in context. God's thought, the essence, manifests in something changing. What is it that changes? It is nothing more than a pair of opposites changing their relation from one which is in balance to one which is out of balance. When anything happens this is what happens. To wish that nothing would happen is to wish a non-existence! So if we wish to be in existence, things will happen. What happens are expressions of God's thought. If we handle what happens strictly on the level appearance, we will be constantly handling crises. But what happens is not arbitrary. The particular possibility realized is the expression of God's thought. The situations we face and have to handle are Divinely chosen especially for us. They are expressions of Divine Beneficence. We can always handle them and we can grow by handling them. By growing we can even learn to handle more difficult balancing situations. The possibilities we create by the balancing we do now lays the foundation for our future.

One could think now that if one does or if one does not do, opposites will come to be out of balance, so what difference does it make if one does not do? This difference between doing and not doing is the difference between life and death. We live, so we do.

One could also think that one should do is act to prevent anything from getting out of the balance that it is currently in. But this too is death. This is the death of striving to hold on to the being of the things as they are now.

Lee writes of this death:

> Anxiety is the state of being unrealized. It is an attempt to maintain the state of being in the process of becoming. It is the constant awareness of one's existence being threatened by becoming. It is

[10]ibid, pp61-62.

> a possibility of losing his security built on his existence. The possibility of threat is a constant reminder of his uncertainty and restlessness. The state of being which he wants to maintain changes to the process of becoming, but he want to cling to it. Thus the being to which he holds is not real, so that it will never be realized.[11]

When we face the changing appearance with the knowledge that this is just the expression of Divine Beneficence, we become faithful. That is we have faith. With faith we see the wholeness of reality. We transcend

> the distinction between life and death, between good and bad, between saints and sinners, or between the Change and the Changeless.[12]

Without faith, we can just intellectualize. Our discrimination and reason will see the parts and not the wholeness of reality. And these parts we will see in conflict, not as complementary parts to something whose beauty is in the balance that can be created. Our failure to create the beauty is our failure to properly exercise our freedom. And this causes our anxiety.

Love is the embracing response to change. For the change brings recognition of separation and when love is the response to the change, then the love brings the experience of union. Here we discover that union is not a static state. Rather, union is a process of separation and return. Union is the process of spiritual breath. Lee writes:

> The Change works in love. It directs the world through love, the inner essence of harmony and unity. The Change without love is chaos and conflict. It is the love that makes the Change complementary and harmonious. The orderly and unifying process of becoming is possible because of love. Love is also creative in the process of becoming. The Change does not repeat the old but renews the old because of love. The creative process of the world is possible because of the interplay of the giving and receiving love. [13]
>
> Love is in a process of becoming. It is not in a state of being. It is in a constant interplay of giving and receiving self. Through the constant giving and receiving self, it can fulfill the lack within the wholeness. Love fulfills the needs of each other. It fulfills

[11]ibid, pp62-63.
[12]ibid, p64.
[13]ibid, p69.

> the other by the self-giving and fulfills the lack of his own by the self-receiving love. Through this mutually fulfilling interplay the Change is constantly operating. Love is more than the sacrifice of one at the expense of the other. One's sacrifice is for the fulfillment of others, and the fulfillment of others is in return for the fulfillment of his. Love deals with the whole process of becoming, the process of the giving and the receiving self. The lover is also the beloved in this process of wholeness. In love the lover and the beloved are not separated. They are united together. Thus to love others is to love oneself. Love is inclusive of all differences, for it is the whole process of becoming. [14]
>
> Love is spontaneous. The process which is not spontaneous is not love. Love moves like the flowing water and the air of the open field. Love does not act upon the premeditated attempt. Love is a spontaneous response to the beloved. It is therefore direct and intuitive. It is not purely rational. It is not motivated out of rational process. No one makes love, but love can make man love others. Love never makes him conscious of himself. It is natural. To be in the process of natural movement man is not conscious of his own self. To be unconscious of his own existence is to be in harmonious union with the one whom he loves. In the process of love one does not notice his own presence. He becomes the part of the beloved, for he is totally participating in the beloved. Because love is spontaneous, the moment of unconscious self is possible.[15]

So love is the response to the presence of Change. It is love which embraces the change and eliminates separation and makes for totality. And what drives love? What drives love is meaning. For it is ultimately meaningful to participate in the fullness of Change. There is no meaning in static existence. Change provides for the possibility of meaning. When Change is not embraced, then we must suffer. For it is exactly then that we do not love and embrace the Change. What provides meaning for us is exactly what provides suffering. Whether we experience it as meaning or as suffering is completely dependent on how we respond to it. Without love, we experience it as suffering. With love, we experience it as meaningful.

Lee writes:

> Meaning is not dependent on the state of being. To be is meaningless. Meaning comes from the Change that changes all things. It

[14]ibid, p70.

[15]ibid, p71.

> is meaningful to change. It is meaningless to be the same forever. Meaning is something which makes it relative; it is not that which makes it secure. What is secure is meaningless, but what is relative is meaningful because of the Change. Anything that is meaningful is related to the Change. The things of the Change are relative. Thus meaning is found in relativity, which is also absolute for relativity is the creation of the Change which is absolute.
>
> Meaning is not found in the things that are external to themselves. It is not in the external manifestation of the Change. Rather it is in the inner presence of the Change in all things. Meaning is found in the inner harmony of all things, that is, love. Thus meaning is of love. What is of love is meaningful. Love makes things meaningful. Things that are meaningful must participate in love. To be in love is to be in harmony with the Change. Thus to be meaningful is to be one with the Change.
>
> Meaning is found in the wholeness. What is fragmentary and partial is not meaningful. Meaning deals with the totality of things. To be meaningful is to be a part of the whole process of becoming. To participate in the process of becoming is to find meaning in life. Isolation from the changing process is the life of meaninglessness, and participation in the process of the Change is to find meaning in life. Meaning is not realized in the analytical and discriminative reasoning, but in the undifferentiated continuum of wholeness.[16]

And what is this wholeness? This wholeness is experienced when we act to reveal the Godly Light. Revealing the Light is not for the satisfaction of our ego, and not for the satisfaction of ourself, but is in satisfaction of Divine service, the Divine service to which we are committed. When the ultimate motivation of our feeling, our desires, our actions is Divine service, then we participate in and mystically experience this wholeness.

---

[16] ibid. p.79.

Appearances

Nothing is what it appears to be,
Yet everything is its appearance.

As it is with appearance,
So it is with nothing,
And so it is with everything.

Each appearance always means more than itself
Since it is a symbol for an essence that
Transcends its own givenness.

Each appearance covers a deeper appearance;
The web of relationships between the cover and the covered
Develop the meaning of each of the involved appearances
And fulfills their essences.

Every action energizes a complex of appearances
And each energized appearance gives life to
Those appearances it covers.

When the energies of all activated appearances
Chain together and lovingly reinforce one another
In a way consistent with the highest good,
The highest good is experienced.

When the energies of all activated appearances
Do not chain together,
They tug against each other
In a way that prevents their fulfillment
And feeds external forces.
Disharmony and disruption are experienced.

Without the appearances in which I clothe
The unknowable nothing I am in material existence,
I cannot materially be.

Even though I choose, create, and am responsible for the appearances,
I am not these appearances.

Hence, nothing is what it appears to be,
Yet everything is its appearance.

Running and Returning

Eternity in motion we call time.
Eternity in unity we call fullness.
Fullness in time we call Eternity.

Running is experiencing eternity in motion.
Returning is experiencing eternity in unity.
Drawing near the Divine is experiencing fullness in time.

To run and return is to do in the world,
And then in our most inward understanding,
Grasp the Godliness in all.

This sublime experience of running and returning,
Constantly deepens us bringing us closer to God.

Our world view changes.
Our inertia decreases.
Our drive for security decreases.
Our courage strengthens.
Our energy increases.
Our skill increases.

For in realizing the true nature of our creativeness,
We are more able to free ourselves
From the limits of our current reality.
We become more willing to change it,
By changing ourselves,
And let it be transcended to a more Godly state.

We give ourselves to God:
Our wants become God's wants.
Our will becomes God's will.
And this is a most wonderful sublime experience.

In amazement we want to cry out in joy.
But there are no words.
So in awe we remain silent,
Running and experiencing eternity in motion,
Returning and experiencing eternity in unity,
Drawing near to the Divine
And experiencing the fullness in time.

The Many And The One

The many is the darkness
By which the One can be concealed.

The many is the brightness
By which the One can be revealed.

By our faith does the many become bright and meaningful.
By our faithlessness does the many become dark and meaningless.

For without faith, there is only the many,
With faith, there is only the One.

When there is only the One,

> The physical is the external manifestation of the One.
> The spiritual is the internal manifestation of the One.

When there is only the One,

> Our thoughts are directed solely towards God.
> Our heart is a mirror by which the Divine
> Is reflected inward.

When there is only the One,

> Our consciousness dwells in God.
> Our heart is a projector by which the Divine
> Is emanated outward.

The mirror reflects inward,
The projector radiates outward
Every Divine quality.

Know that Divine essence is manifested through attribute.
Understand that the One is veiled by the many.
See God in all creatures, in everything.

When there is only the One.

There is only the One.

Only the One.

One.

God's Mirror

The world is a mirror of infinite reality.
Let us see it!

The world is a temple of majesty.
Let us revere it!

The world is a region of Light and Peace.
Let us reflect it!

The world is a mysterious depth of Darkness.
Let us reveal what is hidden in it!

The world is the rhythm of God's singing,
Let us hear it!

The world is a depth of Divine joy.
Let us feel it!

The world is a stage of the infinite.
Let us play in it!

The world is our delicate and sweet nourishment,
Let us taste it!

The world is our garden of blooming flowers.
Let us dance in it!

The world is:
Such awesome magnificence,
Such refinement and sensitivity,
Such delicacy and fragrance.

The world is such a blessing:
A mirror of the infinite!

The Winds

Western Winds: Malchut

Western winds are brisk,
But their bite is only surface deep.

There is a difference between my inner
Or spiritual state of being
And the personality or character
Of the individual I choose to be.

What this character does and how this character feels
In each circumstance is under my control.

I create and control the character
By how I define the character to be,
And by the goals I set the character to pursue.
Whatever kind of life the transitory character pursues,
There are no guarantees of success.
Whatever happens, the character is bound
And confined to feel the feelings
Consistent with its own essence.

When the character encounters situations in which the character
Cannot succeed in being and fulfilling itself,
In which the character cannot successfully pursue its goals,
The character becomes irritated, anxious, depressed, and
A sick puking feeling engulfs the character.

The western winds create turmoil,
For the character's essence is threatened.

Eastern Winds: Tiferet

Eastern winds are soft and deep,
And they feel everything.

The state of the character and the feelings of the character
Have nothing to do with my internal state of being.
The character can relentlessly pursue, be aggressive,
And be disappointed.
And I watch and enjoy this character in its motion.
I can understand this character's feelings,
I can understand why the goals must be pursued:
For the pursuit is a manifestation of the character's essence.
It has no other way of expression, but to be what it is.
In whatever it pursues, there are no guarantees of success.
Whatever happens, the character is bound and confined to feel
The feelings consistent with its own essence.
But I, I am not this character.
I am the creator of this character.
My being is not tied to what happens to the character.
My being is not tied to the dramatization the character acts out.
It is only tied to why I create the character the way I do.
All of life's encounters are situations and opportunities
To which my internal state of being responds and expresses itself
By choosing the motivation for making the character
Be what it is.

Commentary

My most fundamental freedom
Is the internal state of being I choose.
My body physically manifests
The character I create by my internal state of being.

The life encounters of the character
Provide neutral physical situations
Which are opportunities of expression
For my inner state of being.

My inner or spiritual state of being
Is not hurt when the character gets hurt.

Nor is it happy because the character is happy.

My inner state of being channels the Godly life force
Which permits me to center
And maintain a concentrated focus.
In this state of centered concentrated focus,
There is peace, quiet, solitude,
A general feeling of love,
And affirmation for the way everything
Inner and outer works.
Should my internal state of being
Identify with the character
Rather than view the character
As an expression of the focus
Of my center of attention,
The roller coaster life of the character
Will create a roller coaster turmoil
In my inner state of being.
Such turmoil hastens the breakdown of my body
Which simultaneously houses
My inner being
And is the character's physical body.

Therefore, I try not to center
On any outside circumstance of the character's life
Which I would rather be different than it is.

I center on defining the motivation

For each of the character's actions,
Whatever the circumstance the character may be in.

Because I affirm the way it all happens,
I naturally and fullheartedly accept
All the character's circumstances.

It is like traveling down a road.
People can cut in front of me,
Or stop their vehicle in the middle of the road,
Preventing me from going on.
Sometimes I get frustrated.
Sometimes things get bumpy.
Sometimes they get tight.
Sometimes I get lost.
Sometimes the road may even disappear.
Each such situation
I view as an opportunity
To exercise an expression
Of my internal state of being.

I may want the character to do things one way.
But circumstances may force a different way.
I may want the character's friends to be different than they are.
In each such case, I learn and relearn the lesson:
That it is not the external situation which matters,
But it is what motivation I have
For making the character say what it says,
For making the character feel what it feels,
For making the character think what it thinks,
That really matters.

I learn and relearn
That what I have no control of
Cannot ultimately matter to me.
That what I do control
And have complete responsibility for
Is the expression of my internal state of being.

Wanting anything but my internal state of being
To be different than it is
Must create inner turmoil
In place of the peace and joy I seek to express.

Changing the state of my internal being,
Is the easiest and most immediate thing I can do.
I center my focus and will it to be
As I desire it to be.
If I engage in this kind of expression
Of my spirituality with a full heart
And if my attention is focused on one and only one thing,
Then just as a liquid takes the shape of its container,
My inner being takes the state
Which my focus of attention centers for it
And holds it in.

From this point of view,
I understand that regardless
Of the difficulty, desirability, or undesirability
Of the present circumstances of the character,
There is nothing in the character's world
Which is against me.
It is all a neutral ground
In which I can express
My spirituality and experience and observe
The expression of the spirituality of others.

Who are these others?
It is not the characters my character interacts with.
It is the being behind those characters.
They and I are all part of the One: One God.

Walking The Path

My will creates the role
For the character my body plays
In the physical world in which it lives.
I manifest myself through this character.

My will individuates my I
By identifying and attaching the I
To what it chooses.
This act separates me from what I am.
I do it to become conscious of who I am.

I can attach myself to the many:
To my body,
To the role my character plays,
To my character's feelings,
Its acts of love or power.
And I can attach myself to the One
Which we all are.

In this existence I live
By and through these attachments.

The world in which my character lives is largely uncontrollable.
Pushing and shoving circumstances do confront my character,
Sometimes making things pleasurable,
And sometimes making things miserable.
I can easily become absorbed
In the highs and lows my character experiences.

I humble the character
So that it is small gentle and open in its world.
This makes it easier for the character
To give without expecting a return,
To recognize its mistakes,
And flexibly change what
It thinks or does according
To the world circumstances
In which it finds itself.

I make the I identify with my will,
That in me which is creator,

Rather than my character,
Which is my creation.
This makes it easier for me
To realize my freedom,
Change my attachments,
And bless my character and its situation.

Then I expand the I so that it embraces the entire world.
So doing, I rediscover who I am
While walking the path
Of eternal ecstasy.

The One Wills

The One Wills.

The One eternally Wills to give
The greatest of all gifts: a manifestation of itself.

The One is what the One Wills to become.
What the One Wills to become manifests in the world.
What manifests is not the One,
But is of the One.

Since what manifests is not the One,
It is separated from the One.
Since it is of the One,
It stands alone
As a free spiritual and physical
Manifestation of the One.

In the image of the One,
I am a manifested individualization of the One,
Who may receive, fulfill and bless that which is given.
This individualization, my real self,
Is the essence of my Being.
It is my soul.
Each moment, its activities are to complete itself
By receiving, fulfilling and blessing
That which has been given.

To receive that which is given,
I tune my consciousness to the Divine.
I create the personality and activity
Of my character who
Acts, thinks, and feels through the body
That lives in the world.
I write its lines.
I will it to do what it does.
I make it feel what it feels.
I tune its thoughts.
I animate its being.

To fulfill that which is given,
I recognize each situation

The character finds itself in the world
As a neutral situation which sets up
An open possibility, an opportunity, and a responsibility
To so align myself with the One
That, in love, do I discover what the One would will to do.
Then I make my character to do
What has been so discovered.

To bless that which is given,
I make my character always feel
Thankful so that it blesses its situation
And its life.
To do this, I make it focus all its attention on me,
Its creator and silent watcher, rather than the chatter
Of the world in which it is.
And I focus my attention
On the Divine One rather than
The predicament of the character.

If I do not receive, fulfill, and bless
That which has been given
I create a character
Which has not become a manifestation
Of a completed individualization.

In receiving, fulfilling, and blessing
That which has been given,
Each moment I return, in love, to the One
The completed manifested individualization,
Thereby making the Giver a Receiver
And making the receiver which I had been
The giver which I have just become,
An eternal part of the One.

Meditation

Dear God, give ear to my heart.
Help me glow with inner devotion,
So that my thoughts and deeds take wing,
Ascending to your throne.

Let me draw near Thee.
Even through appearances of separating walls,
Let me draw near Thee.
For I know that You fill the world.
And no place is devoid of Your Presence.

Let my songs below
Arouse songs above.
Let my songs topple appearances
And reach through to Thy essence.

Let me bind my soul to Thy Divine Liveness
Flowing through all of creation.
Let me join myself to each.
Serving as the connection
That carries this flow back to Thee.

Let my faith reach through all,
Knowing that every day is a new creation,
Knowing that all worlds are new,
Knowing that I have just been reborn.

Transforming and Unifying

In order to be a giver, the giver has to have the intention to give and the capability to give. Then there has to be a receiver who regards what is given as valuable, appreciates receiving what is given, and can work with what has been given.

For the receiver to appreciate what is given and to regard what is given as valuable, the receiver cannot already have what is given. But, the receiver must have a physical, emotional, or mental space, an emptiness, in which to accept, put or place what is given, through which what is given can be used or developed.

There are many times in which we are given something we do not want. To receive it require us to make space and in effect transform ourselves to form the space in which to completely receive and develop what is given. This process is the process of transforming and unifying.

In one sense, the transforming and unifying processes are very simple. In another sense, they are very subtle and require explanation.

We are given something. To receive it, we must make a place for it within us. This means we have to accept it and go beyond ourselves to find a way to transform or develop it into the greatest good, the greatest benevolence that we are able to bestow through it. This process of going beyond how a thing initially appears to be is how we can be like the Infinite. For infinity is that which is beyond any beyond. To accomplish the transforming to go beyond where we are, requires attentiveness, restriction, creation, and development on our part.

In each moment we are given a situation. If we already have a place to receive the situation, we will judge that a good has been given and we easily accept it, put it in its place, and without thought or effort are able to work in or through the situation with joy developing what we must in the moment.

If we do not already have a place to receive the situation, we shall judge that a bad has been given and we will want to reject it. But our pushing it away will not make it go away. In each successive moment it will stay outside us and push on us, scratch on us, and find some way to bore itself inside of us, leaving us with the consequences of having pushed it away. This is the lingering experience of the bad.

But if we we are attentive, we can restrict ourselves in a way that creates an opening in our inner space. If we put in the effort to transform this opened space to receive the situation so that it can be developed, then the situation which was initially received as a bad will be received as a good. And a unification results. The unification is between what is given and the space we made to receive it.

Consider a concrete example: a city orchestra. The orchestra's sole purpose is to bring the beauty and harmony of music to its city. To economically survive, it must raise additional funds beyond its performance admission fees. This is the situation given. To receive this situation, each year the orchestra engages in fund raising activities setting a goal of some $200,000 to be raised.

During one year the fund raising is not going well. In fact, it is a disaster. The orchestra is close to having to declare economic bankruptcy which will cause it to go out of existence. Just days before the orchestra will have to close down something happens. This represents the situation of the current moment.

What happens is that two young brothers, ages 8 and 9, who take violin lessons and aspire to some day play in an orchestra, hear about the financial difficulties of their city's orchestra. What can they do? They decide that all the money they saved up in their piggy banks should be sent to the orchestra to help out. So they contribute their 153 pennies to the fund raising effort.

Now imagine the situation for the orchestra. It only has funds for a few more days of existence and it needs to raise $200,000, and nothing is coming in the mail on this day but this one envelope having .53.$1 What kind of irony is this? What is God doing playing such a cruel game, to mock the fund raising effort by providing on this day ?53.$1 This is the thought rejecting or pushing away what has been given.

The fund raising disaster with the 53.$1 received this moment represents the bad that is given. Recognizing what has been received without any judgement, and, therefore, without any emotional reaction, constitutes the attentiveness. The fund raising campaign which was designed to receive many checks of $100 each receives instead only 153 pennies. That "fund raising how to" which was already designed and implemented represents the space already filled and occupied. The 53.$1 represents that which is pecking at the orchestra to get inside and occupy an appropriately formed space.

How can an appropriate space be formed for ?53.$1 Well, from the monetary point of view, the 53.$1 represents just about nothing. But from where the 53.$1 comes and what it represents to the givers, this is everything.

The transforming and unifying take place as follows. Just as the 53.$1 represents everything to the givers, for it is the total savings of the two young brothers, so must the 53.$1 and the giving young brothers represent everything to the orchestra. To do this the orchestra develops a human interest story. They get the news media to broadcast pictures of the two young brothers practicing on their violins. The story shows the piggy banks which had contained the 53.$1 and concludes with the simple declaration the young brothers make of how important music is for them.

This change in fund raising strategy constitutes, first, a restriction of the previous strategy and, second, a creation of a new strategy. The creation of the new strategy cannot come about until there is first a restriction of the previous strategy. The restriction opens the space, thereby leaving some emptiness. The creation of the new strategy forms the empty space which fully receives the 53.$1 from the giving young brothers. The broadcasting of the human interest story develops and uses what has been received.

The transforming and unifying completed, the next moment begins. And what happens? The donations begin to be mailed in. And in a few day's time, the entire $200,000 that the orchestra needs is raised. Thereby, the gift of the ,53.$1 which represents a deficiency in its initial context, becomes a fullness in its final context.

From this example we see how transforming and unifying become the means to fully and completely receive what is given in a situation of deficiency, commonly understood as a bad situation. Through transforming and unifying, the giver becomes a complete giver, the receiver becomes a complete receiver, and there is great joy and delight in the good that is brought about through the unification.

Giving and Receiving

In every interaction there is a giving and receiving that happens simultaneously at multiple levels. Each level of giving and receiving constitutes a unification. The base level is when the giver gives what is to be given and the receiver receives it. The giver gives a vessel and the receiver receives and takes possession of the vessel being given. This is how conventional street wisdom understands giving and receiving.

This base level is not unified when the transaction is not complete. That is, when the receiver does not take possession of what is given. But this is not the only level. For the giver gives not only the vessel but also gives a spiritual essence along with the vessel. The spiritual essence is the essence of the giving from the giver's point of view. The essence is relative to the giver's intent of the giving and to how the giver hopes the receiver will be able to utilize the given vessel for both physical and spiritual purposes.

When the receiver receives what is being given, the receiver not only receives the vessel, but also the spiritual essence of the what that is given, as this spiritual essence is interpreted by the receiver. The receiver indicates to the giver that the receiver has received the spiritual essence of the giving by giving back to the giver the acceptance of the giving. For the receiver in accepting what is given is also giving this acceptance to the giver. To complete the unification at this level, the giver must accept the receiver's acceptance.

This second level of unification is easily understood by thinking about the usual social etiquette in the giving of a gift. The giver gives and the receiver receives. The receiver says something like, "Thank you, it is just what I wanted." indicating such an acceptance of what is received that the receiver's acceptance constitutes the receiver's giving to the initial giver. Then the initial giver says something like "Enjoy and use it well." This constitutes the initial giver's acceptance of the receiver's giving the receiver's acceptance of what the initial giver has given. Because the receiver has already told the giver that "it was just what I wanted," the giver's statement, "enjoy and use it well," completes the unification.

There is yet another level to the giving and receiving that is not necessarily apparent from the verbal social interaction. This level is a higher spiritual level and has to do with the more global understanding and intent of the giver and the receiver. This level is activated when the giver understands and feels that the giver has been the receiver of Divine giving and as an agent of the Divine, the giver chooses to pass along the giving. The giver's understanding and feeling that the giver has been the receiver of the Divine giving constitutes the giver's acceptance of the Divine giving. For this the giver thinks or says a blessing. This level is unified when the receiver understands that the giver is in fact acting as an agent of the Divine and therefore, the receiving is not just a physical/spiritual receiving, but a spiritual receiving from the Divine as well. For this the receiver thinks, says or gives a blessing. And this constitutes the receiver's acceptance of the Divine giving.

There is one higher spiritual level. This is the level at which both giver and receiver make a conscious choice to understand everything happening in their lives starting from the point of receiving the Divine giving. This is the level of so aligning their individual will with the Divine will that the giver and receiver are always evaluating and understanding, not from their individual point of view, nor from their family's point of view, nor even from their country's point of view. But they are evaluating and understanding from the point of view of the universe, a point of view beyond themselves. The issue is whether the act in question will in its direct and indirect effects be of greater benefit to one's self and the universe than any other act that could be undertaken. We call this level the level of cosmic consciousness. It carries with it a central internal calmness and peacefulness, an equanimity, that cannot be shaken. For at this level, the ego is nullified. There is no reason for reacting or getting upset about the seemingly "bad" things that others are doing. They are understood as the hand of the Divine setting up situations that make possible the revealment of the highest level of virtue that we, to whom the "badness" is done, are capable of revealing.

Such situations are precisely those situations in which a Divine spiritual giving is occurring. The issue is whether we are open for receiving it. When we are, we are deeply thankful for this possibility. We complete the unification by completely receiving what has been given and we do what must be done to reveal the highest level of virtue that we can. Our center is not moved and we experience indescribable delight.

How does this work practically? Let us consider the situation where the giver forces the receiver to receive something the receiver does not want to receive. The receiver may not want to receive the given vessel itself or may not want to receive the spiritual essence given along with the vessel, or may not want to receive either. For example, what happens when the giver gives an insult to the receiver or when the giver-merchant overcharges the receiver-buyer. In this kind of giving the receiver has been wronged and the unification of the complete-giving/complete-receiving will not happen, unless the giver or receiver act in an especially virtuous way.

Let us look more closely at the situation. The giver was in control. The giver was the initiator and was responsible for the wrong doing given to the receiver, a wrong doing that has a dimension of vessel and has a dimension of spiritual essence. And the receiver must receive the bad thing the giver is giving. How can the receiver completely receive such a giving? For the giving by nature was not complete.

When we receive a bad thing we feel bad for having been wronged. An injustice was done. The insult was unwarranted. The insulting statement not only is a put down, but it is not true. The overcharging merchant is not fair. We engaged in the transaction with an implicit understanding that the exchange was to be a fair exchange. We had no desire to get from the merchant either more than what is proper or less than what is proper for the fair exchange. We, the receiver have been violated by the bad thing given to us. In every situation that we do not completely receive, we will feel in some sense violated. As the receiver, our problem is to completely receive a violation! How can we do that?

We must think as follows: We must think that the giver of the violation is the hand of God. Perhaps the "bad" we have been given is spiritually similar to a "bad" that we had earlier given to someone else. Or perhaps it is a "bad" that we were about to give to someone else. Or perhaps the "bad" we have been given carries within it a spark of Godliness and the situation has been expressly created for us to provide an opportunity to bring into action a virtue, to manifest a quality of Godliness, that is beyond what might be ordinarily expected. For example, God might have expressly created the situation for the purpose of providing us the possibility to manifest the appropriate virtues which would help the giver become a complete giver. If we, the receiver, could do this then since the giving would be complete, the receiving would be complete and the violation and hurt would disappear from existence. Or God might have expressly created the situation for the purpose of providing the possibility for us to manifest the virtues required to enable us to be a complete receiver of what the hand of God has given us. This latter case commonly happens for the purpose of bringing the realization to the receiver that the receiver must change the way the receiver makes judgements so that the the receiver might learn how to be more correct in interpreting the spiritual essence of what has been given.

Our first step to completely receive the "bad" is to accept the hurt and move on to take action which brings out the sparks of Godliness concealed within the "bad". When we do this, something very interesting happens. Because we begin to engage in an action to reveal Godliness, the hurt goes away. It dissolves.

Initially it is the ego within us that yells: hurt! hurt! hurt! Return hurt to that which has hurt us! Withdraw from, isolate, or destroy that which has hurt us! But as soon as we engage in an action to reveal Godliness, the ego becomes occupied as the coordinator of the activity we engage in to bring out and reveal the spark of Godliness. The ego which had been yelling hurt no longer is in existence.

With respect to the giver, there is more. For the giver has not become a complete giver. To facilitate the giver becoming a complete giver the receiver must try, in a proper way, to make sure that all the facts are known by the giver. For perhaps if the giver more fully understands what actually happened, the giver would have acted differently. Doing this properly means that the receiver must fully understand the giver's assumptions, perspectives, and framework of operation, so that the receiver can engage a dialog with the giver and do so from the giver's point of view. This kind of dialog can straighten out mistakes made by the giver at the level of vessel or mistakes by the giver at the level of spiritual essence of what is given, or mistakes made by the receiver relative to the interpretation of the spiritual essence of what has been given.

If this level of action does not work, the receiver may initiate actions which catalyze social pressure to be put on the giver to right the wrong. Or the receiver may take legal action. Or the receiver may take no further action and just drop the situation. But for the receiver, the essence of what the receiver does is to help facilitate the giver to become a complete giver and for the receiver to become a complete receiver.

Now let us consider the situation from the point of view of the giver. How does the giver completely give in this situation in which the giver has just given a "bad" to the receiver. First the giver has to come to a recognition that a "bad" had been given. When the giver recognizes that the giver has made a mistake, the giver must immediately stop any other activities that involve making the same mistake and resolve not to make similar mistakes in the future. Then the giver must right all the similar past wrongs that the giver committed. This level is the level of nullifying the "bad" vessel of what had been given. The amount overcharged the receiver must be returned to the receiver. The giver must explain to the receiver that the giver made a mistake and that the giver will not make the mistake again. The insult must be taken back. The giver must go to the receiver and explain to the receiver of the insult that the giver no longer feels about or judges the receiver in such an insulting way.

Finally, the giver tells the receiver that the giver is sorry for having made the mistake. This is important because it is the action which undoes the giver's intent of giving the "bad" to the receiver and/or undoes the receiver's judgement that the giver had intended to give the "bad" to the receiver. This level is the level of nullifying the "bad" spiritual essence of what had been initially given.

The receiver completely receives the giver's taking back of the giver's mistake and completely receives the giver's regrets by telling the giver that the receiver has forgiven the giver. Everything now is all right. All is forgiven. The giver receives or acknowledges the receiver's acceptance of the giver's taking back of the giver's "bad" by telling the receiver "thankyou for understanding."

This level is the level of unification that completes the nullifying of the "bad" spiritual essence of what had been initially given.

This process of recognizing the mistake, stopping all other such mistakes that may be in process, resolving not to make such future mistakes, righting all the wrongs, and telling the receiver of the mistake that the giver is sorry constitute the process of *return*. The "bad," both the vessel and its spiritual essence, which had been brought into existence is completely taken out of existence. It is returned to non-existence. We call this process *Teshuvah*, תְּשׁוּבָה, whose literal meaning is *reply, answer, response, rejoinder, return,* or *repentance*. It is related to the root שׁוּב, meaning return, and associated with the passage:

> And you shall *return* unto the Lord your God and hearken to His voice according to all that I command you this day, you and your children, with all your heart and with all your soul.[1]

When we have made an error by incompletely giving or incompletely receiving, תְּשׁוּבָה is our response, our reply, our answer, to the repair which must be done. It is the way we can recover from a mistake and continue on the mission of completely receiving and giving that we are called upon to do. Completing this mission is our return to a greater nearness to God, to a greater God-consciousness.

---

[1]Deuteronomy .30:2

The Good and Evil Prompter

> *When a man's ways please the Lord, he maketh even his enemies to be at peace with him.*[1]

About this verse Rabbi Simeon of the Zohar says:

> How greatly is it incumbent on man to direct his path toward the Holy One, blessed be He, so as to observe the precepts of the Torah. For, according to our doctrine, two heavenly messengers are sent to accompany man in his path through life, one on the right and one on the left; and they are also witnesses to all his acts. They are called, the one *good prompter*, and the other *evil prompter*. Should a man be minded to purify himself and to observe diligently the precepts fo the Torah, the good prompter who is associated with him will overpower the evil prompter, who will then make his peace with him and become his servant. Contrariwise, should a man set out to defile himself, the evil prompter will overpower the good prompter; and so we are agreed. Thus when a man sets out to purify himself, and his good prompter prevails, then God makes even his enemies to be at peace with him, that is to say, the evil prompter submits himself to the good prompter.[2]

> *For he will give his angels charge over thee, to keep thee in all thy ways.*[3]

About this verse Rabbi Judah of the Zohar says:[4]

> And when a man enters upon an evil way and then forsakes it the Holy One is exalted in glory. Hence the perfection of all things is attained when good and evil are first of all commingled, and then become all good, for there is no good so perfect as that which issues out of evil. The Divine Glory is extolled and extended thereby, and therein lies the essence of perfect worship.[5]

---

[1]Proverbs, .16:7

[2]*The Zohar*, Vol. II, Harry Sperling, Maurice Simon, and Paul Levertoff (translators), The Soncino Press, London, 1978, p.65.

[3]Psalms .91:11

[4]Harry Sperling, Maurice Simon and Paul Levertoff (translators), *The Zohar*, Vol. II, The Soncino Press, London, 1978, p. .134

[5]*The Zohar*, Vol. IV, Harry Sperling, Maurice Simon and Paul Levertoff (translators), The Soncino Press, London, 1978, p. .125

As Job kept evil separate from good and failed to fuse them, he was judged accordingly: first he experienced good, then what was evil, then again good. For man should be cognizant of both good and evil, and turn evil itself into good. This is a deep tenet of faith.[6]

The Zohar teaches:[7]

According to the companions, the moment a child is born into the world, the evil prompter straightway attaches himself to him, and thenceforth brings accusations against him, as it says,

Sin coucheth at the door,[8]

the term *sin* being a designation of the evil prompter, who was also called sin by King David in the verse:

And my sin is ever before me.[9]

He is so called because he makes man every day to sin before his Master, never leaving him from the day of his birth till the end of his life. But the good prompter first comes to man only on the day that he begins to purify himself, to wit, when he reaches the age of thirteen years. From that time the youth finds himself attended by two companions, one on his right and the other on his left, the former being the good prompter, the latter the evil prompter. These are two veritable angels appointed to keep man company continually. Now when a man tries to be virtuous, the evil prompter bows to him, the right gains dominion over the left, and the two together join hands to guard the man in all his ways: hence it is written:

For he will give his angels charge over thee, to keep thee in all thy ways.[10]

R. Simeon here discoursed on the verse:

---

[6] *The Zohar*, Harry Sperling, Maurice Simon, and Paul Levertoff (translators) Vol. III The Soncino Press, London, 1978, p. .109

[7] *The Zohar*, trans. Harry Sperling, Maurice Simon and Paul Levertoff, (translators), Vol. II, The Soncino Press, London, 1978, p. .134

[8] Genesis .4:7

[9] Psalms .51:5

[10] Psalms .91:11

> When a man's ways please the Lord, he maketh even his enemies to be at peace with him.[11]

> How greatly, he said, is it incumbent on man to direct his path toward the Holy One, blessed be He, so as to observe the precepts of the Torah. For, according to our doctrine, two heavenly messengers are sent to accompany man in his path through life, one on the right and one on the left; and they are also witnesses to all his acts. They are called, the one, "good prompter," and the other, "evil prompter." Should a man be minded to purify himself and to observe diligently the precepts of the Torah, the good prompter who is associated with him will overpower the evil prompter, who will then make his peace with him and become his servant. Contrariwise, should a man set out to defile himself, the evil prompter will overpower the good prompter; and so we are agreed. Thus when a man sets out to purify himself, and his good prompter prevails, then God makes even his enemies to be at peace with him, that is to say, the evil prompter submits himself to the good prompter.[12]

Rabbi Jose of the Zohar teaches:

> When a man walks on the right side, the protection of the Holy One, blessed be He, is constantly with him, so that the other side has no power over him, and the forces of evil are bowed before him, and cannot prevail over him. But as soon as the protection of the Holy One is withdrawn from him by reason of his having attached himself to evil, that evil gains the mastery and advances to destroy him, being given authorization to take his soul.[13]

R. Eleazar expounded there the verse:

> Know therefore this day and consider it in thine heart (לְבָבֶךָ) that יהוה is God is heaven above and upon the earth beneath; there is none else,[14]

as follows.

---

[11] Proverbs .16:7

[12] /it The Zohar, Harry Sperling, Maurice Simon and Paul Levertoff (translators), Vol. II The Soncino Press, London, 1978, p. .65

[13] *The Zohar*, Vol. II, Harry Sperling, Maurice Simon and Paul Levertoff (translators), The Soncino Press, London, 1978, p. .290

[14] Deuteronomy .4:39

The use of the form (לְבָבְךָ) instead of לִבְּךָ suggests a plural, "hearts"; and what Moses meant was this:

> If thou desirest to know that יהוה and אֱלֹהִים are one within the other and both are one, consider thine own 'hearts,' i.e., thy two inclinations, the good and the evil, which are fused one with the other and form a unity.[15]

R. Abba expounded in a similar way the verse;

> *Thou shalt love* יהוה thy God with all thy heart (לְבָבְךָ) and with all thy soul and with all thy strength.[16]

> "The holy unification," he said, is intimated here, and an earnest appeal is made to man to declare the unity of the Holy Name with a supreme love; viz. "with all thy heart" לְבָבְךָ, as above), i.e. with the right and the left with the good and the evil inclinations; "and with all thy soul," with the soul of David, which is placed between them; "and with all thy strength," i.e. to unite in mind the two Names (יהוה and אֱלֹהִים) in the transcendental sphere which passes all understanding. This is the perfect unification through the true love of God. Jacob, the unifier of sides (attributes), represents symbolically this love.[17]

R. Isaac of the Zohar explains the meaning of the verse:

> *He delivereth the poor from him that is too strong for him.*[18]

He says:

> This means that God delivers the good prompting from the evil prompting; for the evil prompting is hard like stone, whereas the good prompting is tender like flesh. What does the evil prompting resemble? When it first comes to associate itself with a man it is like iron before it is placed in the fire, but afterwards, like iron when it is heated and becomes wholly like fire.[19]

---

[15] *The Zohar*, Vol. III, Harry Sperling, Maurice Simon and Paul Levertoff (translators), The Soncino Press, London, 1978, p. .88

[16] Deuteronomy .6:5

[17] *The Zohar*, Vol. III, Harry Sperling, Maurice Simon and Paul Levertoff (translators), The Soncino Press, London, 1978, p. .90

[18] Psalms .35:10

[19] *The Zohar*, vol. V, trans. Harry Sperling, Maurice Simon and Paul Levertoff (translators), The Soncino Press, London, 1978, pp. .359-360

R. Hiya said:

> The evil prompting is at first like a wayfarer who comes to the door of a house and, finding that there is no one to stop him, goes into the house and becomes a guest. Finding that there is still no one to stop him he takes liberties and acts as the master until the whole house is subject to thim. From where do we learn this? from the story of David and Nathan. Nathan first said, "There came a traveller to the rich man" – a mere traveller who passes the door without any intention of staying there and meaning to proceed on his way. So the evil prompting when it first approaches a man prompts him to a petty sin, being still but a chance visitor. Then the text goes on, "to prepare for the guest that came to him." So the evil prompting incites him to greater sins one day or two days like a guest who stays in a house one or two days. Next it says, "And dressed it for the man (אִשׁ) that was come to him" (the word אִשׁ meaning *master* as in "the man, the master of the land"[20]). So the evil prompting becomes the "master of the house" in respect of the man, who is now bound to his service, and he does with him what he likes. Hence a man should ever carry about with him words of Torah in order that the evil prompting may be subdued by them, since there is no opponent of the evil prompting like words of Torah; wherefore it is written, "And these words shall be upon thy heart (לְבָבְךָ that is, upon both thy promptings, the good prompting that it may be crowned with them and the evil prompting that it may be subdued by them.

R. Judah asked:

> Why does the good prompting need them?

He replied:

> The good prompting is crowned by them, and the evil prompting, if it sees that a man does not repent nor seek to study the Torah, goes above and points out his guilt.[21]

---

[20]Genesis .42:30

[21]*The Zohar*, Vol. V, Harry Sperling, Maurice Simon and Paul Levertoff (translators), The Soncino Press, London, 1978, p. .360

The Onion

There she is. She is busy in the kitchen preparing the family supper meal. She acts with carefulness and love, transforming the uncooked food into a nutritious tasteful meal. Such an important activity, the making of food that nurtures, providing each one with the daily nourishment required to serve God.

There He is. He is busy in the study, preparing a Torah lesson for his class which meets after dinner. To do the preparation he has to relearn the lesson at his level and then determine the essence of the lesson at the level of his students so that what he teaches can be fully received and understood.

God looks down at these two of his children and sees how each is involved with Torah. How beautiful. The Holy One can do nothing but smile with a Divine smile.

As the Divine smile fills heaven with delight, the Holy One of All Being says, "Look!" At this very moment all of Heaven direct their attention to where God is looking. For they know that in the next few moments, in the mystery of all mysteries, a world is about to be created or about to be destroyed. All the angels in the seven Heavens focus in. They do not want to miss a single detail.

As they look, they see that she is preparing a new kind of sauce for the chicken. She has cut up garlic and other spices and is just going to the cupboard to get an onion for the sauce. She opens the cupboard and when she reaches in to get an onion she finds there are no onions.

What is she to do? The sauce without the onion would not be the correct sauce. The sauce must have an onion. But now she has no time to go to the grocery. She has about an hour left to when dinner is to be served. The chicken and vegetables are cooking and need watching and stirring. What can she do? She runs to her husband. She tells him "I need an onion!"

Now the moment that all heaven is waiting for is about to occur. All the angels take their places. The hidden legions of angels who are the destroyers take up their weapons of destruction. The hidden legion of angels who are the makers take up their tools of making. The singing angels take up their places in their respective choruses. Just as he is about to respond to his wife, in this split second, his evil prompter and good prompter walk up to each other. They look at each other, eye to eye, honoring each other with the greatest of love. Then they take a step away from each other and give each other a final nod. So, so deep this final nod of acknowledgement. On the one hand the nod of each says to the other to "play your role well", and on the other hand the nod also says "peace."

In an instant the prompters are at his side. As the good prompter whispers to him, he becomes aware of the thought

> She is preparing food for the holy purpose of nourishing us so that we may continue to do mitzvahs and serve God with joy and vigor. Now she lacks only an onion to make the special sauce she prepares perfect. I must put aside my lesson and run to get her the onion.

As the evil prompter whispers to him, he becomes aware of the thought

> I am preparing a Torah lesson and she wants me to interrupt this preparation and get an onion! Can't she make a different kind of sauce? Surely, there are alternatives.

And now comes the moment of action, the moment that will be forever recorded in eternity: Will he harden his heart and push her away by suggesting an alternative sauce? Will he be obdurate to her impassioned pleading to get an onion for her or will he embrace her and run to the grocery and get for her the onion? If he pushes her away a world will be destroyed and the angel choruses will begin to wail. If he restricts his preparation and embraces her by getting her the onion, a world will be created.

What magnificence in this moment! For an onion, a world can be destroyed. For an onion, a world can be created. But we come to understand the deeper mystery. The onion was only the vehicle, a neutral vehicle that created the conditions under which Godliness can be made manifest, depending on his action.

He chooses to get the onion. The making angels start working with their tools as God creates a world. The chorus angels joyously sing. The evil and good prompter look and each other and smile in delight.

But what was so momentous, so deep, in this situation? It is just an ordinary situation, an everyday common family occurrence. Let us look closer and see what is really going on and why this ordinary situation is one under which Godliness can be made manifest.

On the surface, when she comes to him, she comes in apparent need of an onion. She comes as a receiver. And he, by getting her the onion, responds to her as the lover. He is the giver. She is the receiver.

But there is a deeper level. When she comes to him as the receiver, she comes as the beloved. She gives him the gift of her belovedness. For when she comes as the beloved, she gives him the gift of the opening through which he can be her lover. Spiritually she therefore comes as the lover. She is the beloved in one way and the lover in another way. And as she comes to him, God walks with her. As she stands as the beloved, God stands as the beloved. As she stands as the lover, God stands as the lover.

On the surface, when he gets the onion for her, he is the giver and therefore the lover. But the action of getting her the onion is an acceptance of her role as the beloved. When he accepts her gift that she is the beloved, his acceptance makes him a receiver and therefore the beloved to her. Thus he too is both the lover and the beloved.

And this is the reason why his choice to get the onion creates a world. For in that action there is a unification that brings Godliness into their lives. She becomes his lover and his beloved.

He becomes her beloved and her lover. He becomes a complete giver. She becomes a complete giver. He becomes a complete receiver. She becomes a complete receiver. In the world of Assiya, the world of action or making, what has just happened unifies the four letters of יהוה, the tetragrammaton, the unpronounceable name of God Transcendent. In the deep mystery of creation, actions which unify the four letters of יהוה, create a world. For such actions make manifest in our lives that God the Transcendent is God the Immanent.

י He beomes a complete giver
ה She becomes a complete giver
ו He becomes a complete receiver
ה She becomes a complete receiver

When there is love, the lover gives love and receives love. The beloved gives love and receives love. There are two givers. There are two receivers. The two loves are intertwined in complete giving and complete receiving. The Hebrew word for love is אהבה. It has gematria of .13 The intertwined loves, two loves which are one, doubles 13 to 26 and 26 is the gematria of the Eternal transcendent source יהוה. This is one of the secrets of the Holy name יהוה.

This is the meaning of

> *Listen, Israel. The Eternal* (God the Transcendent) *our God* (God the Immanent) *is One.*
>
> *Listen, Israel. The Eternal,* (God the Transcendent, that which we perceive as beyond) *our God* (God the Immanent, that which we perceive as here) *is One, we can transform that holiness that we perceive as beyond into that holiness that we perceive as here.*

Kavannah: The Intention

Up to this point, we have emphasized that he, the hero of the story, the onion man, had a free choice to get the onion or not. Thus the elements consisted of his free will and his action. We ignore, regarding it as not important for the story, as to whether or not his wife was justified in requesting him to get the onion vis a vis how important was her work versus his work. Making that judgment was not the point to the story. And we described the spiritual consequences of the choices. We did not enter inside the onion man to investigate why he made the choice he did. What was he thinking? What was his motivation? Did he have to struggle to make the choice he did? What was his Kavannah, his intention. Now we will.

Did the onion man just make a utilitarian choice to do the good deed because the consequences of that choice were better. For if he decided not to get the onion, his beloved wife would feel hurt. She might cry. Or she might get angry at him and there would not be peace in the house. Or she might not say anything now, but when at some other time he wanted her to do something she would choose as he did and not choose to do it. So the onion man reasons that the consequences of not getting the onion are clearly negative. So he reluctantly decides to get the onion as this choice had the greater beneficial consequences, the greater utility.

If this is how he reasons, he is certainly ethical and utilitarian. But can we call this deep love? Certainly it is not deep love. It is some kind of a transaction, an exchange. She gets benefits now and he banks her good will to get benefits at some future time, so he gets the onion. Or if he does not get the onion, she is going to make life unpleasant for him and this will cause a deficiency. So to avoid the deficiency, he gets the onion. In either of these cases, his intention is either to avoid a negative transaction or to get for himself something out of the transaction. We would be hard pressed to call this the highest form love. Perhaps a utilitarian love is more the correct term. A utilitarian love is indeed love, perhaps a bit selfish love, but it is not the highest kind of love.

There is another mode of loving, a mode at a higher level. We call this level transcendent love to contrast it with utilitarian love. Transcendent means going beyond and in this case to transcend the self, meaning to transcend the narrow self concern in which ego plays an essential role in transactions which are either selfish or utilitarian. Transcendent love means that the lover recognizes what the beloved would like to receive. And he makes himself available to give to the beloved what the beloved wants to receive. His act of giving to his beloved is not just an act arising from a love commitment. Surely there is a love commitment. And his act of getting the onion is consistent with the love commitment. But it is not just because of the commitment that he gives to his beloved. He is certainly aware of the commitment. But if we ask him is he giving to satisfy the terms of the commitment, he would say no. He would say he simply gives to his beloved because he loves her. Giving to her is an essential part of his expression of who he is. As he is the lover and this is who he chooses to be, he fulfills his role willingly by giving. And by so giving he draws down the Divine light.

Thus, he does not give in order to get. Although when his beloved receives his gift of love, her act of receiving is a giving to him. So he does in fact receive. But he does not give in order to receive or because he knows that he will eventually receive. Even if he is conscious that he will receive, he does not give for the sake of receiving. He gives simply for the sake of giving as that is the correct action on his part to fulfill the person he is and wants to be. And in giving, he does no internal work.

There is yet another level of transcendent love. Perhaps we can say that it is even a higher level. In this level the onion man recognizes his own desires to continue with his tasks and not get the onion. This is the voice of his Yetzer HaRa, his evil inclination. But he reasons that he is after all the lover. This is the reason of his Yetzer Tov, his good inclination. And a lover, if he is to be a lover, must express his love. He must give. He must serve his beloved, selflessly. Otherwise the character he is living or playing is not the character of the authentic lover. He does not evaluate whether or not there are any benefits for him in getting the onion. The only thing that is important is that for him it is a higher priority to express his love for his beloved than to continue with his own work, however interesting or important that work might be.

So at first the onion man is conscious of his own ego desires to continue what he is doing. In essence at the first moment he fails internally. He fails to be the transcendent lover. He has doubts, questions, judgments. But then he recognizes that his role is to fulfill a higher principle: to be a lover and express his love to his beloved. This re-cognition of his purpose is his internal work, his toil. So when he at first fails, he recovers by doing the internal work to change his values that were activating his momentary hesitation, and then he rises to be the lover he truly is. This is the highest level of the dynamics of transcendent love for not only did he love, but he had to do internal work to overcome and transcend an initial hesitation and judgment.

In actual reality, in situation after situation, the transcendent lover sometimes finds himself in one level of transcendent love and sometimes in the other. Regardless, however, he does express himself as the lover, for the sake of loving, and not for the sake of any reward of receiving love from the beloved.

On our individual paths of developing ourselves as the transcendent lover, God gives us different types situations. The situations, although all different, are essential kaleidoscopic replications. At first we might have to do some internal work to express transcendent love. With practice, for this kind of situation, we become able to do it naturally, without any internal work. When we reach that plateau, God gives us a different class of situations. And we have to dig deeper, do more internal work. We may have to change some more values, values that we did not even realize we had. We may have to change the way we think about the situation. When at first we fail, we may feel some negative emotion. In this case we must use intellect to start from first principles about who and how we are. And for the context in which we are speaking the first principle is to be the transcendent lover. When we recognize that we are not there, our consciousness is not there, we make a change in some values or a change in some priorities. We change the way we are judging. We change what we are thinking. We change what we are feeling. We change our consciousness. We move from a mode in which we are momentarily conscious of some deficiency into a mode of giving where the consciousness is full. When we give, we live a fullness and there is no deficiency.

It is this changing something internal, moving from a deficiency to a fullness, that is our work, our internal toil. When we complete this work, a completion that may only take a fraction of a second, we put ourselves in a state of being able to express who we really are and what we really want to be. This fraction of a second of internal work would not be noticed externally. But through the toil we become the transcendent lover, the one who our Divine soul wants us to be. We encounter the hiddenness of יהוה, God transcendent, and engage the dynamics of יהוה. By so altering our consciousness, we draw down a Divine light that is beyond the original creation, a light not even part of the original creation, a new creative light. We unite, in our consciousness and in the spiritual world beyond our consciousness, the letters of the Holy transcendent name.

Complete Receiving

When we receive more than is given,
We appear to others as takers.

When we receive less than is given,
We appear to others as escapers.

When we give more than the situation calls for,
We appear to others as overbearing.

When we give less than the situation calls for,
We appear to others as stingy and weak.

When we completely receive what is given,
We appear to others as uplifting.

We delight.
We bless.

Balanced Receiving

We can receive more than is given.
We can receive less than is given.

If we receive more than is given,
In measure for measure,
The excess of our receiving,
Is given to us by the *other side*.

If we receive less than is given,
In measure for measure,
The excess of what is given,
Nourishes the *other side*.

We can give more
Than the situation calls for.
We can give less
Than the situation calls for.

If we give more
Than the situation calls for,
The excess of what we give,
Nourishes the *other side*.

If we give less
Than the situation calls for,
The deficiency of what is needed
Is made up by the *other side*.

All giving by the *other side*
Sets off side reactions,
Whose purpose is to entice us
To engage in the unholy,
To trick us to turn away from God.

Whenever it appears that the situation
Gives us too little,
We interpret the situation as bad.
And this causes us to suffer.

But within the bad situation,
Hidden within all that comes
From the *other side*,

Is a spark of Godliness.
And it is this spark
That we are called upon to reveal.

The Beloved

The Lover stands before the Beloved,
What do his eyes see?

His eyes are not the eyes of the CNN reporter,
Who sees imperfections:
This is too short,
That is too long,
Here is a scar,
This is out of proportion.

The Lover's eyes see beauty,
Harmony and perfection.

When the Lover talks to his Beloved,
His talk is not short.
His talk never ends.
His talk is not talking,
His talk is singing.
Over and over he sings,
With endless repetitions,
Each repetition unique.

His singing is not his singing.
For they sing together:
One melody two voices,
Two voices, one melody,
Two melodies, one voice,
One voice, two melodies.

When the Lover stands before the Beloved,
He does not stand.
He dances in rhythm.
One move counters another move.
The question of who begins
And who follows is meaningless.
It is a dance of two as one with one.

Now look around and see the Beloved,
She gives life to the earth and all that is on it.
Her spirit is within all,
A part of her is everywhere:

In each of our situations,
All the time, we are never without her.
She sings to us constantly,
She dances with us eternally,
Can you see her?
Are you conscious of her?

She sings see me now!
Can you see me?
Touch me, I am here.
Look in front of you.
Look behind you.
You cannot miss me.
I am the closest to you.

She plays with us,
Constantly transforming,
Yet never changing.

She is present even in the times,
And places we think most ordinary,
Or most devoid of her.
And we marvel when we find her,
Realizing that she had always been present.

For the Beloved stands before the Lover.
Playing, singing, dancing, caressing.
Magically in this world and beyond,
Never to end, never to end,
Never to end.

Revealing The Light

Depending on its source,
An action can appear to reveal the light,
Or conceal the light.

The action I do
Appears to reveal the light,
When my primal intent is
To receive for the sake of sharing.

The action I do
Appears to conceal the light,
When my primal intent is
To receive for myself alone.

No matter what the circumstances,
No matter what any other's intent is,
The light always is and
I always receive the light.
But it may appear to me to be revealed,
Or Appear to me to be concealed,
Depending on my conscious state, on my intent.

Revealment of the Light

- Our affinity to Divinity is the revealments of the Light that we make.
- The degree of revealment of the light can be measured by the degree to which we are pushed to our limits and reach beyond our limits in accomplishing the revealment.
- If revealment of the light were easy, it would not be a revealment.
- If we feel that something happens to us is bad, it means that our own eyes are closed to the light. The teachings of kabbalah tell us that in these situations we should adopt an attitude of one of searching for a way to reveal the light which has been concealed.
- We receive Divine Beneficence to the degree we reveal the light.

Receiving

- Each of us has the capability of learning to receive the Divine Beneficence.
- Each of us has the capability of receiving the Divine Beneficence.
- When we receive the Divine Beneficence, we feel a high and are joyous. Everything is right, as it should be, for we can feel and appreciate the Divine beauty and immanence. We are at peace. We are ecstatic; we are in union; we are excited; we love and feel loved. We say there is a revealment of the light.
- When we are not receiving the Divine Beneficence, we feel sad or depressed or disappointed, or doubtful. We think something is wrong. We do not feel the Divine beauty and immanence. We are not at peace. We feel a separation. We are disturbed and something in us is in turmoil. We are not loving and do not feel loved. We say there is a concealment of the light.

Concealment of the Light

- Concealments of the Light occur to give us the opportunity to spiritually grow in making successively more difficult revealments of the Light.
- Concealments of the Light occur to give us the opportunity to make manifest the closeness we have to Divinity, by making the revealments of the Light.
- Concealments occur to give us the opportunity to manifest the knowledge we have to make revealments.
- Whenever we desire to receive for ourself alone, we create a concealment of the light.
- We receive conditions and situations which are open to be received as concealment to the degree we have caused such situations to others.
- We receive conditions and situations which are open to be received as concealment to the degree that we had not used our free will to cause a revealment of the light in previous such situations. In other words, what we do comes back to us. In this way we can have the opportunity of correcting our incorrect use of free will.
- What happens when we act in a way which creates the possibility of a concealment of the light to another? How can that be viewed as something which by the will of God comes to the other?

  What we do with the intent of causing a concealment, is not, in fact, guaranteed to cause a concealment nor is it ever guaranteed to cause the external conditions we originally intended. So we may be guilty of having the intent to cause a concealment, but the concealment depends both on what external conditions actually come to be set up and the state of the other party upon being exposed to those external conditions. For the one who is receiving the possible concealment, it is an opportunity to manifest the knowledge about making a revealment. And this can be viewed as an opportunity from the Divine.
- We always pay the price for having the intent to cause a concealment.

Transcending

Transcending means going beyond. We transcend when we go beyond where we are in order to be what we are. To go beyond does not mean to go with spiritual separated from material. It means to go: material and spiritual together, in union. So where is it that we are that needs transcending to be what we are?

Plato wrote in Phaedrus:

> The human charioteer drives his horses in a pair; and one of them is noble and of noble breed, and the other is ignoble and of ignoble breed.

The Talmud and the Zohar speak of an Evil Inclination and and Good Inclination.

The Baal Hatanya, the Alter Rebbe, speaks of an animal soul and a Godly soul.

Is it the case that we have such a dual nature? The answer is that the duality is illusion. But we have to talk about the illusion, engage it, in order to be able understand what is beyond the illusion.

The Torah speaks about a tree of Knowledge of Good and Evil.

> *And the Eternal יהוה, God, commanded the man, saying,*
>
> > *Of every tree of the garden you may freely eat, but of the Tree of Knowledge of Good and evil, you must not eat thereof; on the day you eat of it you shall surely die.*[1]

But Adam and Eve ate of the Tree and on the day that they ate of the Tree, God throws them out of the Garden of Eden, a garden of paradise. To die means not being in the Garden of Eden. The lesson in the story: when we participate in the illusion of good and evil, we throw ourselves out of the Garden of Eden.

In Hebrew, Garden of Eden is גן עדן. Garden is גן. Satisfaction is עדן. The Garden of Eden is the Garden of Satisfaction. The verse explaining this is

> *And a river goes forth from Eden to water the Garden, and from there it separates and becomes four main streams.* [2]

Rabbi Glazerson teaches that in the True Reality

[1]Genesis 2:16-17

[2]*Genesis* 2:10

> Eden is the source of blessing. It sends forth its beneficial influence through the channel of the river, and thus grants abundance to the recipient vessel, the garden.[3]

Now what is so bad about eating of the tree of Knowledge of Good and Evil? In Hebrew, Tree of Knowledge of Good and Evil is עץ הדעת טוב ורע. The word used for Knowledge is from the root ידע. This is the same root as used in the verse

> *Now the man knew his wife Eve and she conceived and bore Cain.*[4]

Knowledge as used in the Torah is not just intellectual or conceptual knowledge. Knowledge is the kind of knowledge that is experienced and intimate. To have knowledge of Good and Evil means to have the conscious experience of Good and Evil. Consciousness is internal so this means to internalize Good and Evil. The commandment not to eat of the Tree of Knowledge of Good and Evil means not to internalize Good and Evil. This means not to have a conscious experience of Evil. For what God creates is Good. And to entertain a consciousness of Evil, means entertaining in our consciousness a separation from God. It means entertaining an illusion.

What is this illusion of Good and Evil? From a common sense point of view, good is that which is understood as positive or desirable for self. Evil is that which is understood as negative not desirable for self. But if we perceive evil, then we have created a world for ourselves in which God is not present.

All that happens to us is coming to us by the hand of God. So that when we really see, what we see is full and whole. Everything that God continues to create today, everything even in each of its parts is complete. To eat of the Tree of Knowledge of Good and Evil means to bring into our consciousness the category of God-deficiency, itself a contradiction in terms. Perceiving evil means to bring into our consciousness deficiency in place of the fullness and blessing of God. The blessing of God is the True Reality. In our dealings in the world, there is a part of us that wants us to survive, not just to survive but to win, that wants us to live, that wants to impress into reality our rightness, even if we are not right, a part that only wants to be satisfied with its wants, a part that only sees appearance. We call this aspect of our personality the Ego. It is an essential and important aspect of who and what we are.

But what ego wants, it typically mistakenly wants for us alone, even at the expense of others. When Ego wins, the other loses. Such a game is a finite

[3]Matityahu Glazerson, *Letters of Fire*, Feldheim, Publishers, Jerusalem, 1991, p. 95
[4]*Genesis* 4:1

game. In an infinite game, one plays not to win but to keep the delightful game going. The infinite game is a win-win game. The players do not want to stop the game. The spiritual reality is that what Ego wants for us alone cannot ultimately satisfy us. For it is a finite game. But Ego does not know that. Ego cannot reason.

Ego wants what it perceives that self does not have. So it is attached to that want. And if we are not mindful, we become enslaved to that want. Ego's entry into our consciousness brings in a consciousness of deficiency and the desire to do whatever it takes to satisfy that deficiency.

But there is a difference between the reality that Ego perceives and the True reality. Our True reality is Gan Eden. It is present here in this moment for each person. This is the reality that there is nothing but God. This is the reality that everything that comes from God is blessing and therefore good. So that the moment we perceive that there is deficiency, that there is something that we do not have and ought to have, that is the moment that we separate ourselves from God. This separation is spiritual evil and when we act in that way, we are spiritual evil doers.

King David writes:

How great are Your works, O Lord,
How very profound Your thoughts!
A brutish man cannot know,
A fool cannot comprehend this.

When the wicked thrive like grass,
And all evil doers flourish,
It is in order that they may be destroyed forever.[5]

Evil here means separation from God. Evil doers not only refers to that evil that we perceive that is outside of us, but also to that evil, that separation from God, that we do. This evil comes from inside us. And it is this evil that we must first transcend. The purpose of the perception of evil (deficiency) is that perception of deficiency may be destroyed forever.

The way God creates the world on the one hand provides everything that is needed for our joy and good in living. Recall the verses in Genesis chapter 1:

And God saw that it was good. Genesis 1:10,18,21,25

And on the other hand He does so in a way that makes possible the illusion of deficiency. Hence, Ego's unsatisfied desires.

[5]Psalms 91

Rabbi Glazerson teaches that the force behind the concealment of Divinity in the world is the Evil Inclination, the יצר הרע. The Evil Inclination works by painting over the True Reality. יצר has the same letters as the word צייר, meaning an artist who draws or paints pictures.[6] It is this painting that covers True Reality so that the appearance that is seen on the surface, the deficiency, is nothing more than an illusion. To see True Reality we must go beyond the appearance and get to the essence.

What is the purpose of the illusion of deficiency? If everything is provided, then we have no work to do. If we have no work to do, then what we receive has no value. What we receive has value, when we work for it. We work for it by transcending the deficiency we perceive in our situation. It is this transcending that in the language of the Baal HaTanya lets our Godly soul express itself in the material world. And it is this that brings Godliness into the world.

God made a world in which wherever we look, if we do look closely, there is a hint of His Glory. But if we are not mindful, we will not see. In this case God is hidden. And why is God concealed? So that we can transcend where we are in a way that God becomes revealed. What reveals God? The work we do by our transcending.

Transcending makes the immediate present eternal. What we do is not for any extraneous purpose other than being who we are in the immediate and eternal moment. In transcending we do not have to be somebody. We do not need status. We do not need power. We do not need to be important. We are not clinging to any idea or thing. We do not need to intellectualize or rationalize. We are not attached. We are not controlling. Each person before us is not an object to be manipulated. We are not lusting for the result. Rather, we see the appearance, and we also see the essence carried by the appearance. We just need to authentically be who we really are, relate to the essence, and let God take care of the rest.

Transcendently being who we really are is the complete fulfillment of living; it requires no future result. It is complete in and of itself because we relate to essence and not to appearance. There is no want of something not present because all that needs to be present is present. Each person before us is a holy being. There is unity in action, in space, in time and in consciousness. The future, whatever it may be, is united with the present. For transcendently being who we are aligns us with and brings us closer to the Creator of All Being and this makes us free. True freedom comes from being close to God.

[6]Matityahu Glazerson, *Letters of Fire*, Feldheim, Publishers, Jerusalem, 1991, p. .137

Practice

We are in a situation with another person. We are about to say something or do something. How can we tell whether or not the action we are about to take is one of transcending or one of descending? Hesitate for a moment. Ask the question: if I were on the receiving end of the action I am about to do, would it be equally good to me? Is the action a win-win action. Is it an action that uplifts the other person? Is it an action that is good in and of itself? Will the action result in the other person and myself each becoming complete receivers and complete givers or will it result in a taking or one of us receiving only or giving only?

The Good And The Bad

Whatever can be recognized is recognizable only because there is a distinction between what is it and what is not it.

In order for there to be the holy, there must be the profane. So in order to be able to recognize the holy, we have to be able to distinguish it from what is not holy, the profane. And the very recognition of what is holy, what is closest to God, what is closest to unity, depends on the existence of its opposite. Recognition depends on multiplicity. And so we have the paradox that for unity to be recognizable, there must be multiplicity. And this multiplicity is what gives rise to that which has the appearance of good and bad.

When we recognize that a bad thing happens to us and at the same time remember that everything that happens to us is from the hand of God who only gives Divine goodness, we are put in a situation to make a unification. For in the common frame of reference, the happening is bad. But if this, which has the appearance of bad in the profane frame of reference, comes from God, then it really is good and just, in the holy frame of reference.

And from where do we come to know that everything that comes from God is good: perfect and just? Moses tells the children of Israel:

> *Give greatness to our God.*
> *He is our rock.*
> *His work is perfect.*
> *For all His ways are justice:*
> *A God of truth and without iniquity.*
> *Just and right is He.*[1]

This being so, our holy service consists of finding a higher level reference frame from which we can recognize the happening as good, receive the happening as holy. Thus by our change of attitude we receive the Divine goodness and we change and grow. And by what we then do as a result of this reinterpretation in our higher level frame of reference, we reveal the goodness that was hidden in the bad. We meet the challenge of the suffering of the bad by manifesting a higher level virtue, a virtue that we could not bring into being in any other circumstance but the one we are given. We completely receive that which is given to us and by completely receiving, we return it to its source.

But, if we do not completely receive it, it stays and lingers inside of us causing emotions of hurt and anger. Instead of eating the nutritious meal, we leave

---

[1]Deuteronomy .32:4

the food on the plate. After a time, the food spoils. And its putrification then begins to putrify all that is in contact with it. The anger and suffering then begins to eat us up from the inside, destroying us from the inside out. This results in us getting stuck. Our body gets sick and our mind gets sick and we are stuck in enslavement.

Set before us is life and death.

> *See, I have set before thee this day life and good, and death and evil; in that I command thee this day to love the Lord thy God, to walk in His ways, and to keep His commandments and His statutes and his judgments: then thou shalt live and multiply. And the Lord thy God shall bless thee in the land into which thou goest to possess it.*[2]

We are commanded to choose life. We are commanded to chose the holy, to so love God that we receive all that God gives us. To so love God that we keep all His commandments. We are commanded to rise to a higher level and see the holiness within the profane. We are commanded to make a unification and hold within us the unity of the multiplicity. We are commanded to see the good. Then the Lord our God will bless us in the land of milk and honey.

---

[2]Deuteronomy .30:15-16

The Divine Abundant Goodness

Abundant goodness is that which is Divinely given to us. It comes in two forms: concealed and revealed.

The revealed abundant goodness is plain to see and is immediately enjoyed. There is no struggle to receive it. Although there is an uplifting, there is little of an inherent transcendence of what we have been. This is the goodness which forms the warp of the fabric of our life.

The concealed abundant goodness cannot be plainly seen. It is hidden in the difficulties of its circumstances. Because it is hidden, our revealment of what is concealed facilitates a changing within us. This changing, our growing, is our transcending what we have been. The transcending is internal to us and through it we begin again. In transcending we receive and thereby reveal the Divine abundant goodness. The revealment of the Divine abundant goodness is in the actions we do and the things we say that fulfill the Godliness we are called upon to fulfill. The revealment is what we give to God. In giving to God, we become closer to God. The concealed abundant goodness forms the woof of the fabric of our life.

The concealed abundant goodness and the revealed abundant goodness are One. They come from the same source. They come for the same reason. They come to us from God's love.

In the Fullness of the Moment

From the quiet sereneness of my innermost being
The vitality of the flow
Meets the fullness of the moment
In that deep eternal now.

What mystery!
For this is how and what I am.
The moment beckons
And I respond in love.

What completeness!
The moment exists
To receive all that my love has to give.
And what does it give?
But a joyous sharing of my being
And the vitality of the flow.
By giving everything, I hold nothing.
And in having nothing, I have everything.

The outer circumstances set the stage
And clothe the moment with people.
Sometimes the garments are the crowns of friendship
And the pearls of romance.
Other times they are the hard cloak of competition,
The dagger of power or the poison of domination.

Know that the inner central sereneness
Can never be hurt by the garments,
That it has no possessions
And requires not anything other than itself,
For itself is not itself alone and separated,
But is its oneness with God.
Therefore it is its own fulfillment
And can only shine in love.

My consciousness can know of that soulful connection to God,
Through its identification with God.
Making it one with the inner central sereneness.
Then the actions it directs the body to do
Are naturally ethical and compassionate.

The actions shine in love.

The playful flow encounters the clothed moment
In joyous abandonness
To express its immortal essence
And be the celebration it is.
Thereby it meets the fullness of the moment
In that deep eternal now.

The Sefirot

There are ten Sefirot, סְפִירוֹת, and they are the means by which we understand how Being is expressed. Expression means to press out. Expression of being develops through ten stages: כֶּתֶר crown, חָכְמָה wisdom, בִּינָה understanding, חֶסֶד loving-kindness, גְבוּרָה strength, תִּפְאֶרֶת beauty, נֶצַח victory (eternity), הוֹד glory, יְסוֹד foundation, and מַלְכוּת kingdom. These are the ten Sefirot. As everything in the universe is an expression of God's being, everything has the internal structure of the ten Sefirot.

It is not by chance that the word סְפִירוֹת is related to the English word spirit.

S	P	I	R	I	T
סְ	פִ	י	ר	וֹ	ת

The singular is *Sefirah* (סְפִירָה). It means *counting* or *numeration*. It is related to words like: סֵפֶר, which means *book*; סְפָר, which means *border, frontier*, or *border district*; סִפּוּר, which means *story, tale*, or *narrative*; סְפֵירָה, which means *sphere*, and סַפִּיר, which means *sapphire*.

The Zohar calls the Sefirot crowns.

> The Holy One, blessed be He, has produced ten holy crowns above where with He crowns and invests Himself, and He is they and they are He, being linked together like the flame and the coal.[1]

Rabbi Kaplan explains the essence of the *Sefirot*:

> The *Sefirot* are generally referred to as *Midot*, which means literally "measures" or "dimensions," and by extension, attributes or qualities. It is through the Sefirot that God limits His infinite essence and manifests specific qualities that His creatures can grasp and relate to. As such, the Sefirot act variously as filters, garments or vessels for the light of *Ain Sof*, [the endless light] that fills them.
>
> The term *Sefirah* (סְפִירָה) itself derives or is related to the Hebrew *Saper* (סַפֵּר), meaning "to express" or "communicate," and *Sapir* (סַפִּיר), "sapphire," "brilliance" or "luminary." It is also related to *Safar* (סָפַר), meaning "number," *Sefar* (סְפַר), "boundary," and *Sefer* (סֵפֶר), "book." In essence, all of these are related concepts and point to the *Sefirot* as having two basic functions. First, the *Sefirot* are

[1] *The Zohar*, Vol 5, (III, 70a), trans. Maurice Simon and Harry Sperling (London: Soncino Press, 1978), p. .66

> *Orot*, Lights or Luminaries that serve to reveal and express God's greatness. Secondly, they are *Kelim*, Vessels that limit and delineate God's infinite light, bringing it into the finite realm of number and boundary.
>
> This distinction answers a basic question dealt with by the Kabbalists. Are the *Sefirot* essences of the Divine or are they vessels of the Divine? In other words, are the *Sefirot* ten windows through which we can perceive the Divine or are they ten tools that God uses to direct the world? The Ari answers that both are true on different levels.[2]

The *Sefirot* are the forces and vessels through which God fashions all worlds. They are the vehicles for the Revelation of God's will. And because we are created in the image of God, the *Sefirot* are simultaneously the forces and vessels through which we fashion all our worlds. They are the vehicles for the revelation of our will.

But the Sefirot are more than vessels. The vessels carry the light. The appearance reveals the essence. So when we speak of the Sefirot as vessels, we are looking from the outside inward. When we speak of the Sefirot as light, we are looking from the inside outward.

The earliest written commentary of the *Sefirot* is in *Sefer Yetzirah, The Book of Formation.*

> By means of thirty and two surprising hidden[3] paths of wisdom Yah, Lord of Hosts, God of Israel, Living God, God Almighty, awesome and holy is his name, hollowed out and thereby created His universe within the three borders of idea, order, and expression.
>
> Ten ineffable *Sefirot* twenty and two foundation letters: three mothers, seven doubles, and twelve simples.
>
> Ten ineffable *Sefirot* from the counting of the ten fingers, five that are against five, and the unique covenant oriented in the center like the word of the tongue and like the word of the pudenda.
>
> Ten ineffable *Sefirot*, ten and not nine, ten and not eleven. Establish understanding in wisdom and be wise with understanding. Examine inside them and probe through them. Station and speak to the Creator and return the maker to His foundation.

---

[2] Aryeh Kaplan, *Inner Space* (Brooklyn, NY: Moznaim Publishing Corporation, 1991), p. .40-41

[3] and individual or personal

> Ten ineffable *Sefirot*, their ten measures which are nothing compared to their finish: profoundness of beginning and profoundness of the end, profoundness of good and profoundness of evil, profoundness of above and profoundness of below, profoundness of east and profoundness of west, profoundness of north and profoundness of south. Only One Master, God, faithful King, governs all of them from his Holy habitation forever until eternity.
>
> Ten ineffable *Sefirot* whose appearance is like seeing lightning flashing. And their purpose has no limit to them. And His word in them is overflowing and transforming. And according to His longed for decree, they will run and in the presence of His throne prostrate themselves.
>
> Ten ineffable *Sefirot*, their end inherent in their beginnings, and their beginnings in their end, like a flaming fire bound within a burning coal. Because the Master is singular and there is none second to him, then in the presence of the One, what can you express?

The ten Sefirot are part of the Tree of Life which consists of ten Sefirot and twenty two letters making up the thirty two paths of wisdom discussed in Sefer Yetzirah. These thirty two paths of wisdom also correspond to the thirty two times verbs with אֱלֹהִים as the subject are used in the first chapter of Genesis.[4]

The tree is represented in a geometric arrangement with the ten Sefirot as circles and the twenty two letters as links between the circles. In this geometric arrangement the circles are on three vertical columns. Proceeding from top to bottom, on the right column is חָכְמָה wisdom, חֶסֶד loving-kindness, and נֶצַח victory. On the left column is בִּינָה understanding, גְבוּרָה strength, and הוֹד glory. On the middle column is כֶּתֶר crown, תִּפְאֶרֶת beauty, יְסוֹד foundation, and מַלְכוּת kingdom.

Between pairs of some of the circles there are channels connecting them. There are three horizontal channels, seven vertical channels, and twelve diagonal channels. The three horizontal channels correspond to the mother letters א, מ, and ש. The seven vertical channels correspond to the seven double letters ב, ג, ד, כ, פ, ר, and ת. The twelve diagonal channels correspond to the twelve single letters ה, ו, ז, ח, ט, י, ל, נ, ס, ע, צ, and ק.

The dynamics of the expression of being has three pillars: the pillar of expansion, the pillar of contraction, and the pillar of balance. These three pillars are the three columns of the Tree of Life. The right column is the pillar of expansion. The left column is the pillar of contraction. The middle column is the pillar of balance.

---

[4]Zohar Chadash, p.112.

The early Kabbalists understood the ten Sefirot as ten windows by which we can understand God's actions in our world. Since we are created in the image of God, the ten Sefirot are ten windows by which we can understand our own consciousness, emotions, and actions. Our exploration of the ten Sefirot will be from this point of view.

In Kabbalah, the first three Sefirot are called *Mochin*, מֹחִין, which literally means brains. It stands for what can be collectively understood as the intellect. The last seven Sefirot are called *Midot*, מִדוֹת, plural of *Midah*, מִדָּה, which literally means measure. The kind of measures associated with the last seven Sefirot are measures of being human, measures of character. The kind of measures can be more easily understood by the phrase *Midah Tovah*, מִדָּה טוֹבָה, which literally means *good measure* and can be understood as virtue, and the phrase *Midah Ra'ah*, מִדָּה רָעָה, which literally means *bad measure* and can be understood as vice.

The first Sefirah of the intellect, our inner reality, is כֶּתֶר crown. It represents the dimension of our readiness: that aspect of our consciousness that is our becoming and free will. The process in this Sefirah is the activating of our will: That which we will. To exercise our will, we have to be ready and open to receive the immediate and eternal moment, which is the Divine above us. Our readiness and will opens the way to wisdom, *Hochmah*.

The second Sefirah is *Hochmah*, חָכְמָה , wisdom. The letters of חָכְמָה can be rearranged to form the phrase כח מה, literally meaning *power of what*. The power of what is the potential of what can be. When an idea comes to us as a direct flash of insight or a flash of intuition, the sense that we have is a sense of the whole with the intricacy of the details and structure not given and not worked out. It is a direct non-verbal knowing. If we do not pay attention to the insight and begin to work out details to actualize the insight, the insight will soon be forgotten.

Why is this called wisdom? Because when we have a flash of insight, we are opening ourselves up to a higher wisdom. What we receive from this higher wisdom is the insight. This is easily understood: we say that we have an insight when we become aware of the insight as it comes across of the screen of the mind. But we did not plan or think the insight. We just became aware of it by tuning ourselves to the right opening. Tuning ourselves to the right opening is wisdom. Wisdom impregnates Binah.

The third Sefirah is *Binah*, בִּינָה , understanding. Binah means to understand or work out plans and details. Binah takes the insight of חָכְמָה and develops the details. Binah is a vessel that surrounds the insight of חָכְמָה so that the essence of the insight can transform into something publicly communicable. The details now become a limited bounded form or shape of the idea. What happened was that a sense that had all kinds of possibilities became an instance. It became crystalized into a thing of reality, although not yet in physical form. The Kabbalists use the analogy of the pregnant mother making a baby.

The Sefirah חָכְמָה , Wisdom, corresponds to the non-verbal all-at-once intuitive knowing. It is the place that can be sought but is not disclosed. What is disclosed is through the Sefirah בִּינָה , which corresponds to the verbal analytic and linear reasoning aspect of understanding. From this point of view, בִּינָה is light since it can be readily seen in a public manner. But חָכְמָה , is private and cannot be seen in a public way. It is darkness. Darkness precedes light. We connect to חָכְמָה in mystery.

Once our will is set, we open a channel to the above and we draw upon wisdom, that flash of insight, hopefully associated with a Torah correct thought, and we realize the expressed essence of the reality we are given. We call this undifferentiated realization of the essence *insight* or *idea*. This is the action of the Sefirah חָכְמָה wisdom. We then develop the essence-idea into its particulars, its logical components and inter-relationships and come to as full an integration of the reality as we need in order to feel and chose the mode of how to express our feelings. The development of these particulars and their integration into an interpretation of the situation is the action of the Sefirah בִּינָה understanding. In essence, our interpretation is the basic mental component of our turning toward God or our turning away from God.

Chesed, חֶסֶד, is the Sefirah of out-pouring loving kindness. It is below Hochmah on the right pillar of the tree. It is the Sefirah of emotion extended outward or toward, an emotion of pure, complete and free giving: a giving without conditions and without analytic reason. It radiates beneficence, benevolence, kindness, and love. It functions on the pillar of expansion. When we feel like moving toward something, we are activating Chesed. The Sefirah is called loving kindness because the very nature of loving kindness is a movement toward. Moving toward always has an element in it of boundlessness or expansion. This positive phase of being is to expand. That is why one of the alternate names for Chesed is Gedulah – greatness.

Gevurah, גְבוּרָה, is the Sefirah of strength. It is the Sefirah of emotion extended inward or away, thereby limiting expansion. It is below Binah on the left pillar of the tree, the pillar of contraction. Restriction, severity, discipline, and judgment characterize the action in Gevurah, where lovingkindness must be given with restraint, in accordance with merit, and not in a boundless unlimited form. When we feel like moving away from something, we are activating Gevurah. The Sefirah is called strength because it takes more energy to move away or limit ourselves than to move toward. Moving away or inward always has an element in it of limitation or contraction. The negative phase of being is to limit or contract. Contraction always has an element of limiting judgment and that is why one of the alternate names for Gevurah is Din – judgment.

Both Chessed and Gevurah can operate in a balanced peaceful way through a mediating faculty, the Sefirah of Tiferet, תִּפְאֶרֶת. Tiferet is the Sefirah of beauty. It harmoniously blends Chessed and Gevurah. It is the Sefirah of balanced emotion toward and away. It functions on the pillar of balance and harmony. It is called beauty because when the right mixture or arrangement of two contrasting emotions are created, the result is harmonious and therefore called beautiful. By analogy, a drawing that is all white is not beautiful. A drawing that is all black is not beautiful. A drawing that has a balanced pattern of white within black and black within white is beautiful.

Netzach, נֶצַח, is the Sefirah of triumph, victory or overcoming. It is the extension of Chesed, functioning below Chesed on the right pillar of the tree. In Chesed there is only the feeling of moving toward. But there is no determination to manifest this feeling of moving toward. Netzach is the intent or will to do something about manifesting the feeling of moving toward. It functions on the pillar of expansion. The Sefirah is called victory or overcoming because when we hold on to this determination to do something about our feeling to move toward, we are victorious. We are able to overcome anything that might be in the way of our moving toward.

Hod, הוֹד, is the Sefirah of splendor or glory. Being below Gevurah, it is the extension of Gevurah on the left pillar, the pillar of contraction. In Gevurah there is only the feeling of moving away or limiting. But as in Chesed, there is no determination to manifest this feeling of moving away or limiting. Hod is the intent or will to do something about this feeling of moving away. The Sefirah is called glory because when we hold on to the determination to do something about our feeling of moving away, to properly limit our own tendency to expansiveness, it becomes possible for other people to willingly receive what we might be giving. In Hod, we are in essence giving up our own desire to fill the place of our world leaving some of it available for others to be. This is glory. Hod has a sense of subservience to another's expansiveness.

Yesod, יְסוֹד, is the Sefirah of foundation. It is the balance of Netzach and Hod. In Netzach and Hod, there is the determination to do something, but there is no binding of this determination to an action by means of a plan. Yesod is the binding of the determination to an action, the connecting of the determination to a plan of action, so that the determination to manifest the balance of the feelings of moving toward and moving away comes about. It functions below Tiferet on the middle pillar, the pillar of balance.

Malchut, מַלְכוּת, is the Sefirah of kingdom. It is the extension of Yesod, functioning on the pillar of balance below Yesod. In Yesod, the plan of action has been identified. In Malchut the action is carried out. In Malchut the feelings of Chesed and Gevurah are finally manifested in physical reality by action and deed.

The lower seven Sefirot are sometimes called by the names of the seven shepherds. The first three of the seven shepherds are the three Patriarchs, Abraham, Isaac, and Jacob. The Patriarch Abraham is associated with the Sefirah Chesed, חֶסֶד; Isaac is associated with the Sefirah Gevurah, גְבוּרָה; and Jacob is associated with the Sefirah Tiferet, תִּפְאֶרֶת. The fourth shepherd is Moses, who is associated with the Sefirah Netzach, נֶצַח. The fifth shepherd is Aaron, who is associated with the Sefirah Hod, הוֹד. The sixth shepherd is Joseph, who is associated with the Sefirah Yesod, יְסוֹד. Its code name is *Zaddik* in reference to Joseph, the righteous one who resisted the seduction attempts of Potiphar's wife. The seventh shepherd is King David, who is associated with the Sefirah Malchut, מַלְכוּת, whose very name means kingdom.

Different rabbis have constructed the Tree of Life differently. Figure 1 shows the tree as constructed by Moshe Cordovera who lived 1522-1570 and by Isaac Luria who lived 1534-1572. Figure 2 shows the tree as constructed by the Vilna Gaon, Rabbi Elijah ben Shlomo Zalman Kreme, who lived 1720-1797. Non-Jewish Hermetic Kabbalistic discussions typically show the tree shown in Figure 3.

The Tree of Life

Figure 1: Shows the Tree of Life following Rabbi Moshe Cordovera and the Arizal, Rabbi Isaac Luria.

The Tree itself is a hologram. Each of the Sefirot has the entire structure of the Tree within it. To show a complete picture of the holographic nature of the tree would necessarily involve us in an impossible to do infinite recursion. Therefore, here we will show the Tree at the top level. After we work with it, in the second volume *God Consciousness: Working the Sefirot and Netivot* we show the subtree within each of the lower seven Sefirot and we will work with the seven subtrees. There we have extensive Sefirot exercises to move away from the vices and move toward their virtues. When we complete the Sefirot exercises, we will work the Netivot, the paths. In our path working, we have extensive exercises to resonate with and move toward virtues. We will create seven trees, one for each of the lower seven Sefirot. In the subtree of Cheseds, we will gather together all the Cheseds and their virtues: Chesed of Chesed, Chesed of Gevurah, Chesed of Tiferet, Chesed of Netzach, Chesed of Hod, Chesed of Yesod, and Chesed of Malchut and place them on the tree of Cheseds. The channels on the Tree of Cheseds then connect together Cheseds of the subtrees. We will do likewise for the Tree of Gevurahs, the Tree of Tiferets, the Tree of Netzachs, the Tree of Hods, the Tree of Yesods, and the Tree of Malchuts. In this manner we will have two useful orthogonal representations of the Tree. The tradition in Kabbalah is that everything in existence has the structure of the holographic tree.

Before we begin discussing our first exercise, we will explain a few of the Torah verses from which come the names of the Sefirot. We will then discuss how a government in a democracy functions with the structure of the tree. There are then some additional discussions setting the context for the exercise prayer ritual which will conclude this book.

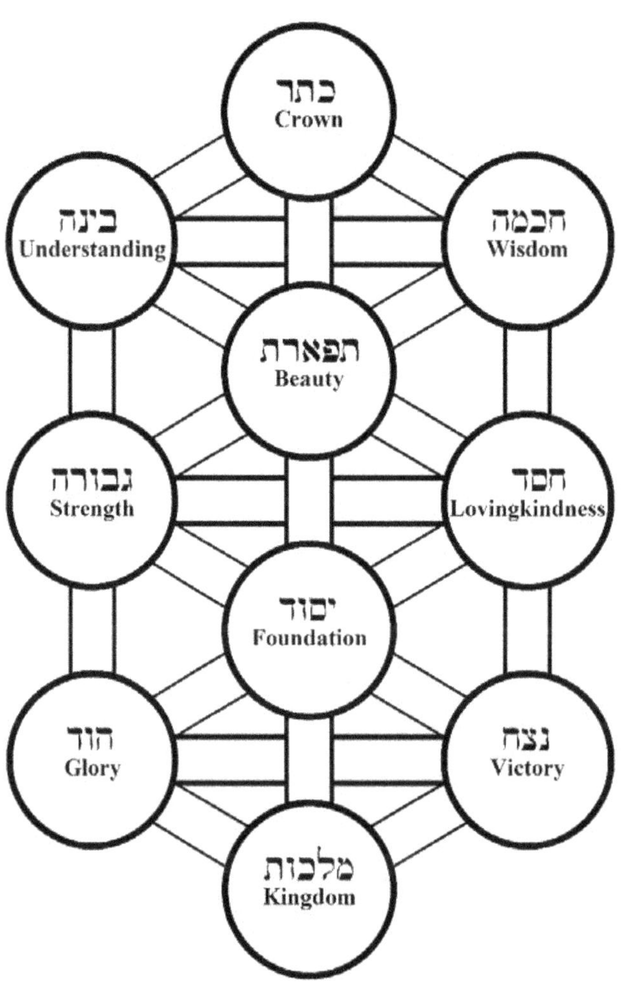

Figure 2: Shows the Tree of Life following the Vilna Gaon.

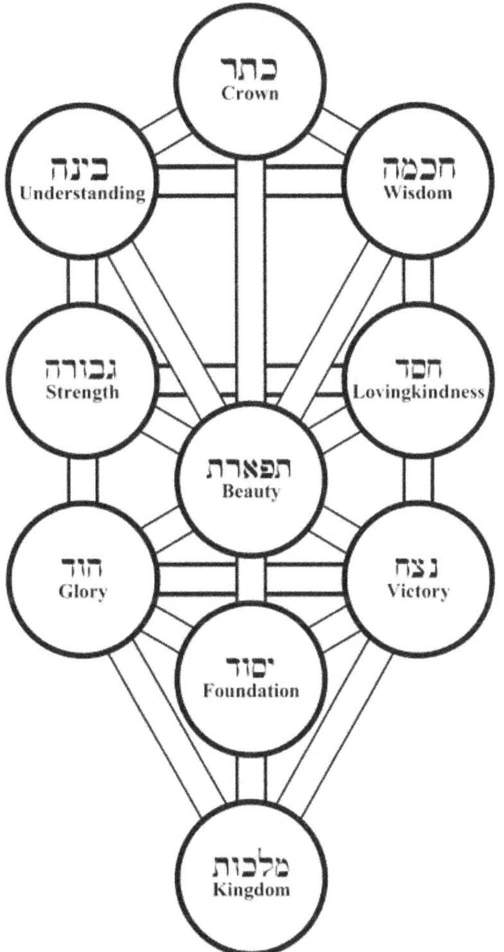

The Tree of Life

Figure 3: Shows the Tree of Life following the Hermetic tradition.

Proclaiming The Name

There is one place in the five books of Moses that there is a direct code phrase for the lower seven of the Sefirot. When Moses begins his last words to the Israelites, he says:

> Give ear, ye heavens, and I will speak; And let the earth hear the words of my mouth.[1]
>
> When I will proclaim the name of the Lord; Give ye greatness. Unto our God, the Rock, His action is perfect. For all His ways are justice. A God of faithfulness, and without iniquity. Just and right is He.[2]

On these verses the Zohar teaches that Moses was referring to the lower seven Sephirot on the Tree of Life. Rabbi Abba gives the following analysis:[3]

Chesed	חֶסֶד	Give ye greatness.	הָבוּ גֹדֶל
Gevurah	גְבוּרָה	Unto our God, the Rock.	לֵאלֹהֵינוּ הַצּוּר
		His action is perfect.	תָּמִים פָּעֳלוֹ
Tiferet	תִּפְאֶרֶת	For all His ways are justice.	כִּי כָל דְּרָכָיו מִשְׁפָּט
Netzach	נֶצַח	A God of faithfulness,	אֵל אֱמוּנָה
Hod	הוֹד	And without iniquity,	וְאֵין עָוֶל
Yesod	יְסוֹד	Just	צַדִּיק
Malchut	מַלְכוּת	And right is He.	וְיָשָׁר הוּא

Chesed is a word of expansion. Greatness is also a word of expansion and its cognate Gedulah, גְדוּלָה, is an alternate name for Chesed. Gevurah means strength. Rock is a metaphor for God. A rock is hard and is a metaphor carrying the meaning of something strong. Tiferet on the Tree of Life is the right balance of Chesed and Gevurah, of expansion and contraction. Justice carries the connotation of the right balance. Netzach on the Tree of Life carries the meaning of victory and overcoming. Faith is the way we overcome. Hod on the Tree of Life means glory. Interaction with communication that is rational and therefore honest is without the iniquity of deceitfulness, the dominant vice of Hod on the Tree of Death. Yesod means foundation and is associated with the biblical character of Joseph, who is considered a Zaddik, a righteous one. Malchut means

[1] Deuteronomy .32:1

[2] Deuteronomy .32:3-4

[3] *The Zohar*, Vol 5, (III, 297a), trans. Maurice Simon and Harry Sperling (London: Soncino Press, 1978), p. .379

Kingdom. The word translated as "right" יָשָׁר is also the word in Hebrew meaning straight. In this phraseology a person who is straight rather than crooked is a right person. The last phrase begins with the word וְיָשָׁר, meaning *and straight*, has the root ישר. Append to this root אל, which is one of the non-erasable names of God, and there results the word יִשְׂרָאֵל , Israel. One of the meanings of Israel is straight to God[4]. This is the kind of person that operates in the Kingdom of God on the Tree of Life.

In the Chronicles I is a verse that describes the lower seven sefirot.

> *Yours Hashem, is the greatness, and the strength, and the beauty, and the victory, and the majesty; for all that is in the heaven and in the earth is Yours; Yours Hashem is the kingdom, and You are exalted as head above all.*[5]

		Yours Hashem is	לְךָ יְהוָה
Chesed	חֶסֶד	the greatness	הַגְּדֻלָּה
Gevurah	גְבוּרָה	and the strength	וְהַגְּבוּרָה
Tiferet	תִּפְאֶרֶת	and the beauty	וְהַתִּפְאֶרֶת
Netzach	נֶצַח	and the victory	וְהַנֵּצַח
Hod	הוֹד	and the glory	וְהַהוֹד
Yesod	יְסוֹד	for all in heaven and earth	כִּי-כֹל בַּשָּׁמַיִם וּבָאָרֶץ
Malchut	מַלְכוּת	Yours Hashem is the kingdom	לְךָ יְהוָה הַמַּמְלָכָה

This verse uses the term Gedulah, *greatness*, as a code word for Chesed. And *for all* is a code phrase for Yesod since in the Cordovera tree and the Arizal tree, to have a path to Malchut, all the Sefirot above Yesod must go through Yesod to get to Malchut.

---

[4]as opposed to crooked with God

[5]Chronicles I 29:11

Government

Government, in a democracy, begins with the will of the people. This will to have a just government opens up the people to receive the wisdom of how to achieve a just government. This wisdom is only a sense, a feel, an intuition. Then the sense gets worked out into the details in the form of a constitution.

> We the People of the United States, in Order to form a more perfect Union, establish Justice, insure domestic Tranquility, provide for the common defense, promote the general Welfare, and secure the Blessings of Liberty to ourselves and our Posterity, do ordain and establish this Constitution for the United States of America.[1]

The constitution gives the power to make laws to the legislative branch of the government. In the United States this is the Congress.

> All legislative Powers herein granted shall be vested in a Congress of the United States, which shall consist of a Senate and House of Representatives.[2]

Rather than considering how the Senate and the House of Representatives work, we take up the orientation of the parties of the members of the Senate and House of Representatives. There are typically two main parties: one is liberal in orientation and one is conservative in orientation. The liberal party functions in the Sefirah Chesed. Their orientation is to provide more services to the people. The conservative party functions in the Sefirah Gevurah. Their orientation is to limit or bound the supply of services to the people. Congress is the place that these two parties meet to negotiate a compromise or balance between their positions. The compromise is the legislative bill that when passed by the Congress and signed by the President becomes the law of the land. Congress acts in the Sefirah of Tiferet.

The law as written in the Congress does not specify the detailed policies and interpretations that must be put in place. These details are left to the corresponding agencies which function under the Executive or Judicial branch of the government. Agencies such as the National Institutes of Health, Health Education and Welfare, Housing and Urban Development are agencies that function on the right side of the Tree in the Sefirah Netzach. These agencies are expansive in the sense that they are givers of services to the people. Agencies such

---

[1] Preamble to the Constitution of the United States

[2] Article 1 of the Constitution of the United States

as the Department of Defense, Federal Communications Commission, Federal Drug Administration, Post Office, Department of Transportation, and Justice function on the left side of the Tree in the Sefirah Hod. These agencies keep order and limit problematic expansion that individuals or corporations or other countries may desire to do for their own profits or benefits.

The agencies are just agencies. Without the civil servants that run and work in them, the agencies can accomplish nothing. The civil servants connect the policies established by the agencies to the particulars of each situation and circumstance. The civil servants function in the Sefirah Yesod.

Finally, the action of the interaction of the civil servants with the people occurs in the Sefirah Malchut.

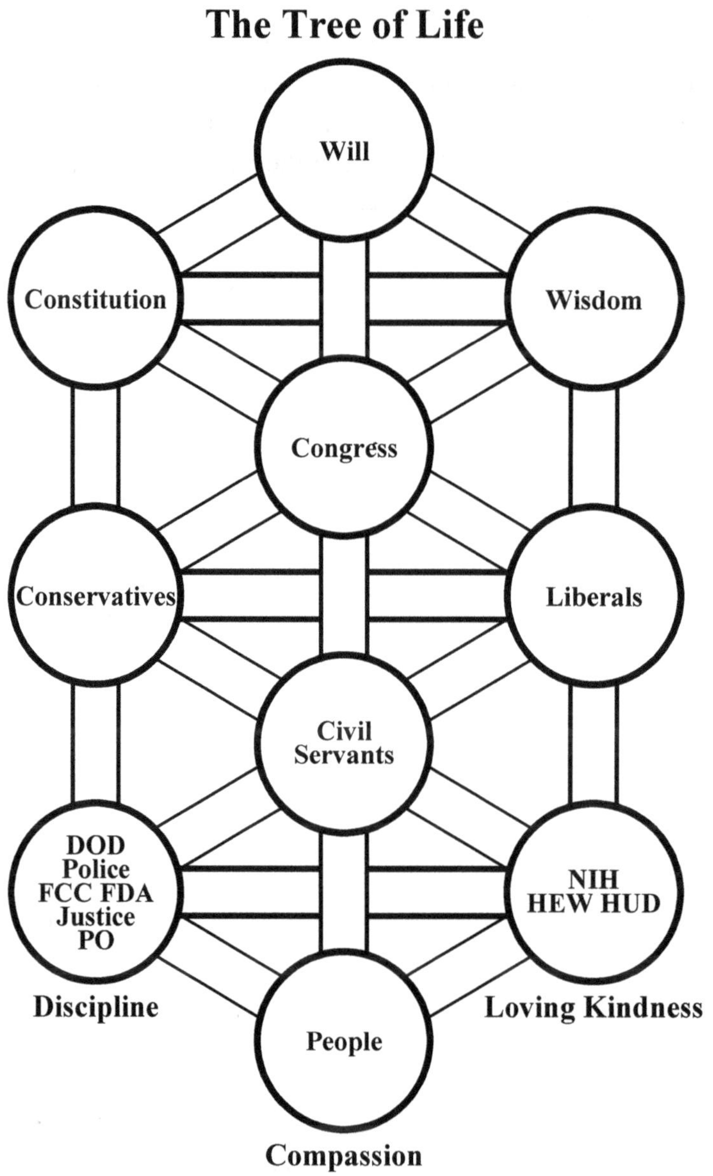

Figure 4: Shows the structure of government organized on the Gra Tree.

Crown, Wisdom and Understanding

Crown, Wisdom, and Understanding,
Light, Essence, and Appearance
Constitute one unified complete whole.
One reality without defect.
One energy.

Primal Intent is the source of life.
It is called will and the Crown.
It is the origin, the true earth.
It encloses everything.
In it there is nonaction.
Yin and Yang are harmoniously blended,
As one without distinction.

Wisdom is Essence.
Outwardly deep and inwardly bright.
Father is strong and vigorous.
Intuition taps this deep well,
Its water forever sharing and flowing downward.
Formless and not material,
It is not constrained.
It is Yang and true knowledge.

Conscious knowledge is Understanding.
Outwardly firm and inwardly flexible.
Mother of the ten thousand myriad things.
Reasoning orders its unfathomable changing Appearances.
As a burning fire, it is forever transforming.
Like fire, it ascends upward.
Formed and not material,
Yet it is limited and constrained.
It is Yin and true intelligence.

Qualified by our choice of a limited state of being,
True Intent closes the channel to Essence.
Essence closes the channel to Appearance.
Appearance separates from Essence.
The One energy divides into three.
The ten thousand myriad things
Tug at one another.
Their essence becomes concealed.
The false is born.
Desire is king.
Emotional turmoil dominates.
The mind is stubborn and disturbed.
Primal Intent no longer maintains affinity with the Light.
The external forces control the Slave.

Qualified by our choice of an elevated state of being,
Primal Intent opens the channel to essence.
Essence opens the channel to Appearance.
Stabilized by will, the mind is free and still,
Concentrated and focused, but not controlled.
There is no lustful desire for results.
Multiple Appearances ascend into one Essence.
One Essence flows into the Crown.
The truth is revealed.
The play is spontaneous.
There are no external forces.
Yin and Yang cleave together.
The circuit becomes complete.
The light returns home.
And the Master delights.

Unification

The descending light
Is the situation we are given.

Our response is our action.
This takes place in Malchut מַלְכוּת .

Our action initiates
The returning light
That ascends up the tree.

Malchut מַלְכוּת transforms to Keter כֶּתֶר ,
And Keter כֶּתֶר is transformed to Malchut מַלְכוּת .

This is the meaning of:
The end is in the beginning
And the beginning is in the end.

In the unbalanced situation
There is a difference
In amount and quality of
The descending spiraling light
And the ascending spiraling light:
There is a deficiency of one
Or an excess of the other.

The *other side*
Makes up any deficiency
And absorbs any excess.

The contribution of the *other side*
Makes a proportionate
Concealment of Godliness
In a present or future situation,
A concealment
We are called upon to undo,
With a corresponding revealment.

In the balanced response,
The descending spiraling light
Couples completely
With the ascending spiraling light.
The two spirals

Wrap around each other perfectly.
Constituting the unification
Of Ehh'yeh אֶהְיֶה and Adonoy אֲדֹנָי .

Levels

There are levels upon levels.

At each level there is appearance.
Behind each appearance there is essence.

At each level Intelligence deals with appearance.
Wisdom deals with essence.

The light of Wisdom animates intelligence.
The light of Will and motivation animates wisdom.

Beyond the Crown of Will and Motivation,
We have no contribution,
We have no kind of inner exertion,
We have no control, influence, or action of any kind.

Beyond the Crown of Will and Motivation,
Is the Endless Light,
Emanating from the Endless.

Beyond the Endless,
is Nothingness,
Neither Being or Nonbeing,
Neither Being or Nonbeing
Or not Being or Nonbeing,
Neither existence or non existence,
Neither existence or non existence
Or not existence or non existence.

Do God's Will

Do His will as if it were your will,
That He may do your will
As though it was His will.

Nullify your will before His will,
That He may nullify the will of others
Before your will.[1]

The first verse tells us not to just do God's will. For we can be doing God's will without a full heart, without the completeness and fullness that we would be doing if it were our will. But that we should be doing God's will as if it were our will.

Now in this process of doing God's will, we will be bringing into manifestation God's will by the actions we perform. We will be doing it completely and fully as if it were our will. But our will still stands as our will and there are things that we have set our will to but not done. Here the verse goes on. That which we have set our will to but have not taken action on, because we are doing God's will, will be done. For the verse says that He may do our will as though it were His will. In other words, without working with effort, what we set our will to but have not done because we are doing God's will, that will be done. It will be done because God will do our will as though it were His will.

Kabbalistically, this is a description from the framework of מַלְכוּת , because the emphasis is on the doing. The next verse says the same thing as the first verse, but it says it from the framework of כֶּתֶר .

The next verse says that we should nullify our will before God's will. And if we do that, the things that others have set their will to which would interfere with our carrying out of God's will, for those things God will run interference for us and block the carrying out of the potentially interfering actions so that the will which we are in the process of doing, God's will, will be done.

---

[1]Ethics Of The Fathers, .2:4

Two Trees

To be with God Consciousness requires that our expressions and interactions be good, joyous, and uplifting. Our interactions must be ones which facilitate a complete giving and complete receiving. In short, our expressions and interactions must be worthy enough to be experienced by others who are in essence God's messengers. We read in the Psalms,

> *Praiseworthy are those whose way is wholesome, who walk with the Torah of* יהוה .[1]
>
> Strive toward the Eternal יהוה and keep His way, and He shall exalt you to inherit the land.[2]

The word used for what has been translated as *way is wholesome* is -תְּמִימֵי דָרֶךְ, literally meaning way or path or manner of wholesomeness or entirety. The verse equates the manner of wholesomeness to the Torah of יהוה . This tells us that that to be involved in the path or manner of wholesomeness is more than the Halacha of Torah. Indeed there is a connotive meaning of תְּמִים as innocent and naive. The phrase תְּמִימוּת-דֵּעִים means complete agreement. So there is a connotive meaning of completeness and agreement. The path or manner of wholesomeness is the path of innocent complete agreement. Agreement means harmony. Harmony means balance. Innocence means purity, lack of scheming for an ulterior motive. The wholesome manner is good in and of itself and not for anything beyond itself. This is the meaning of:

> *You shall be wholehearted with the Eternal* יהוה , your God.[3]

Obviously, actions which in any way cheat, take advantage, or harm another person in all the ways listed by the do not do laws between man and man of the Torah are ways which are not wholesome. But the ways which are wholesome include those as listed by the to do laws of the Torah and include ways which are beyond them, ways which are associated with personality traits.

By developing virtuous personality traits we strive toward the eternal, keeping His Ways and inherit the land. The word translated as land is אֶרֶץ. It can mean earth or land. But in this context it means land and land is a code word for God consciousness.

---

[1]Psalms 119:1
[2]Psalms 37:34
[3]Deuteronomy 18:13

Kabbalah measures each person on seven personality traits. And each of these seven can be subdivided into seven again. Each personality trait has a beneficial aspect and a detrimental aspect. The seven go with the seven lower sefirot on the Tree of Life when they are beneficial personality traits, traits that we associate with virtue. And they go with the seven lower sefirot on the Tree of Death when they are detrimental personality traits, traits that we associated with vice.

Pharaoh dreams.

> *And lo, there came up out of the river, seven cows, well favored and healthy in flesh, and they went grazing in the meadow. And lo, seven other cows came up after them out of the river, ill favored and leanfleshed and they stood next to the cows upon the brink of the river. And the ill favored and leanfleshed cows ate up the seven well favored and fat cows.*[4]

The word translated here as ill favored is רָעוֹת, a word coming from the root רע, the root meaning evil. So it is not the case that we should have pity on the ill favored cows because they are so lean and ugly. The fact is that the evil cows ate the well favored healthy cows.

Joseph's interpretation of Pharaoh's dream is the one relevant to the story of the Exodus over thirty-three hundred years ago and relevant to the Passover celebration. There are, however, other interpretations of Pharaoh's dream besides the necessary one given by Joseph. For each story of Torah has meaning for us in our lives today, beyond the meaning of the history and its associated holidays.

One interpretation relevant for us is that the seven healthy cows are the seven beneficial personality traits. The seven ill favored cows are the seven detrimental personality traits. Both come from the same river. The story tells us that they cannot coexist with each other. The positive ones do not balance out the negative ones.

> *And the thin and ill favored cows ate up the first seven healthy cows. And when they had come inside them, it could not be recognized that they had come inside them; their appearance was as ill favored as at the beginning.*[5]

Not stated in the first telling of Pharaoh's dream, but stated in the second telling of the dream, is that after the seven lean cows ate up the seven fat cows,

---

[4]Genesis 41:2-4

[5]Genesis 41:20-21

the seven lean cows remained lean. This is inconsistent with logic. They should have gotten fattened up. This is what was most confusing to Pharaoh and is the reason that all his wise men could not interpret the dream.

The dream tells us that the reality God created is this way: the seven beneficial personality traits will be eaten up by the seven detrimental personality traits and all that will be left are the detrimental personality traits. Positive and negative do not even produce zero. They produce negative.

And thus God made a Tree of Life and a Tree of Death. Within the Tree of life functions the seven beneficial personality traits and within the Tree of Death functions the seven detrimental personality traits. Beneficial means unification. Detrimental means separation.

> *God has made the one as well as the other.*[6]

A person must know their own character strengths and weaknesses in order to live in God consciousness and be effective in bringing Godliness into the world. If a person has no idea of what he/she lacks and where he/she is deficient, he/she will not know the vices he/she has to correct and of the virtues to which his/her vices must be corrected. In this case all the study of Mussar, the Jewish ethical tradition, will be to no avail, for he/she cannot not recognize himself/herself in the Mussar lessons. And if he/she cannot recognize himself/herself, he/she cannot transcend and change himself/herself.

---

[6] *Ecclesiastes* .7:14

The Tree of Death

The Zohar tells not only of a Tree of Life, but it also tells of a Tree of Death.

> For whoever exerts himself in the study of the Torah and lays hold of it, lays hold of the tree of life; and whoever relaxes his hold of the tree of life, behold the tree of death overshadows him and takes hold of him. So Scripture says:
>
> > *If thou relaxest in the day of adversity, thy strength is narrow indeed.*[1]
>
> signifying that whoever relaxes in the study of the Torah, in the day of adversity, his strength (כֹּחֲכָה= כֹּחַ strength of כּה here, now) is narrow indeed, to wit, the strength of כּה that continually follows on the right of the man that walks in the ways of the Torah, and forms his constant guard, so that the evil power is prevented from approaching him and is powerless to accuse him. But of him who turns aside from the ways of the Torah and relaxes his hold of it, it is said: "narrow indeed is the strength of כּה," as the evil power, represented by the left, obtains dominion over that man and thrusts aside that כּה, so that he has no room to move.[2]

As attachment to the Tree of Life brings spiritual life, attachment to the Tree of Death brings spiritual death.

> Observe that there are two Trees, one higher and one lower, in the one of which is life and in the other death, and he who confuses them brings death upon himself in this world and has no portion in the world to come.[3]

Rabbi Simeon of the Zohar teaches:

> As there are ten Crowns of Faith above, so there are ten crowns of unclean sorcery below. All things on earth are attached either to one side or to the other.[4]

---

[1] Proverbs .24:10

[2] *The Zohar*, Vol II, Harry Sperling, Maurice Simon, and Paul Levertoff (translators) The Soncino Press, London, 1978, p.88.

[3] *The Zohar*, Vol V, Maurice Simon and Harry Sperling (translators), Soncino Press, London, 1978, p.221.

[4] *The Zohar*, Vol IV, Harry Sperling, Maurice Simon, and Paul Levertoff (translators), The Soncino Press, London, 1978, p.410.

The Zohar explains.

> There is a Right above there is a Right below; there is a Left above and there is a Left below. There is a Right above in the realm of supernal holiness, and there is a Right below located in the "other side." There is a Left above in the realm of supernal holiness to procure indulgence for the moon, so as to link her to the holy place and enable her to shine. There is a Left below which estranges the upper realm from her and prevents her from reflecting the sun's light and drawing near to him. This is the side of the evil serpent, who, when this Left of the lower realm bestirs itself, draws the moon to himself and separates her from the upper world, so that her light is darkened. She then causes death to descend like a stream on all that is below; she cleaves to the serpent and departs from the Tree of Life, and so brings death on all the world. At such time the sanctuary is defiled till an appointed time when the moon is repaired and shines again.[5]

The Zohar teaches that the Tree of Death is governed by what we might call the natural powers.

> Observe that the lower grades form a hierarchy, one above the other, and each different from the other, yet all linked and interlocked with each other. So is kingdom separate from kingdom, yet is each linked to the other. All the grades are held, as it were, by one chain of a certain measurement, which in its turn is divided into three smaller chains which reach down and are tied to the stars and the planets, so that each grade is assigned one star or planet. Those stars in their turn operate under the grades above. Every grade has thus charge of its own proper region, and when they diverge, a chain is formed by which each grade is bound to its proper side. The sides of the unclean grades, which are on the left side, diverge all of them into numerous ways and paths and distribute their power to thousands and myriads in the lower world; and in reference to this it was said to Edom:
>
> > Behold, I make thee small among the nations; thou art greatly despised.[6]

---

[5] *The Zohar*, Vol I, Harry Sperling, Maurice Simon, and Paul Levertoff (translators) The Soncino Press, London, 1978, p.168.

[6] *The Zohar*, Vol II, Harry Sperling, Maurice Simon, and Paul Levertoff (translators). The Soncino Press, London, 1978, p.179.

The Midrash on Proverbs discusses the verse:

For he who finds Me finds life
And obtains favor from the Lord.

But he who misses me destroys his own soul;
All who hate Me love death.[7]

The Midrash explains:[8]

> God said: Whosoever is found [studying] words of Torah will find Me in any place [that he seeks Me.] Therefore, it is said, *For he who finds Me finds life.*
>
> God said: Whosoever brings forth words of Torah and teaches them to the multitudes, I too shall bring forth [favor] for him at a favorable time. Therefore, it is said, *Obtains favor from the Lord.*
>
> God said to the wicked: If you sin against Me, do you think in your souls that I suffer any loss? It is yourselves who suffer loss! Therefore it is said, *He who misses Me destroys his own soul.* Not only that, but you think in your soul that you are gaining life for yourselves – you are only gaining death for yourselves! Therefore it is said, *All who hate Me love death.*

Figure 5 shows a new geometry of the tree and is the one with which we will work. This tree is the outermost vice structure of the tree of death. In this tree, each Sefirah is labeled with its dominant vice. The tree as drawn on in the figure is the two dimensional flattened form of the tree. The 3D structure can be seen formed by the top four Sefirot, Keter, Hochmah, Binah, and Tiferet. They form a regular tetrahedron with Keter as its apex. This is the simplest of the five platonic solids. Next there is a regular four-sided pyramid with Tiferet at its apex and Chesed, Gevurah, Netzach, and Hod at its base. Then there is an upside down regular pyramid with Yesod on its bottom and Chesed Gevurah, Netzach, and Hod at its base. The double pyramid is actually an octahedron, one of the five platonic solids.

The tree of death is a tree of spiritual and ethical depravity. The vice in Keter is self will. That means the will is directed to benefit self only, even at the expense of somebody else's detriment. With our will set to benefit ourselves, the channel of insight we open ourselves to also becomes selfish. The vice in

[7] Proverbs .8:35-36

[8] The Midrash on Proverbs, Burton Visotzky (translator), Yale University Press, New Haven, 1992, pp.47-48.

Hochmah is self intuition. That means that Hochmah is open for intuitive insights about benefiting self exclusively. This leads to the vice in Binah, which is self understanding. Here self understanding does not mean understanding of self, but more akin to understanding things for one's selfish benefit.

The vice of Chesed is an unbalanced lovingkindness directed toward self. We call this insatiableness because whatever one does for oneself, it is not enough. Insatiableness leads to an insensitivity toward others, especially when there is an expectation that the other will provide you with something.

He has a tendency for Insatiableness.

Insatiableness is the quality of character inclining one to an unending desire and excessive absorption and addiction in the pleasures of self. Insatiableness includes gluttony, drug addiction, intemperance, ravenousness, narcissism, selfindulgence, and voraciousness. Insatiableness over-indulges the body at the expense of the mind and soul. There is too much love of self and not enough energy for the love of others.

With insatiableness, there is lessened sensitivity to others to the point of inconsiderateness. And when anyone tries to guide an insatiable one to lessen the insatiableness, it provokes a fiery anger. He has a tendency for Insatiableness.

Insatiableness is the quality of character inclining one to an unending desire and excessive absorption and addiction in the pleasures of self. Insatiableness includes gluttony, drug addiction, intemperance, ravenousness, narcissism, selfindulgence, and voraciousness. Insatiableness over-indulges the body at the expense of the mind and soul. There is too much love of self and not enough energy for the love of others.

With a consciousness of insatiableness, the vice of Chesed, there is lessened sensitivity to others to the point of inconsiderateness. And when anyone tries to guide an insatiable one to lessen the insatiableness, it provokes a fiery anger.

Insatiableness The quality of character which inclines one to have excessive desires that can never be satisfied.

With a consciousness of angriness, the vice of Gevurah, there is a strong pushing the other away in angriness. Strength here is misapplied as an anger force against the other because the other is not meeting one's expectations and needs.

Angriness The quality of character which inclines one to an emotional feeling of strong displeasure against the person who acted in a way that displeased us.

Once the habit forms of getting angry at others who are not attending to us the way we want, we fall into an arrogance consciousness, the vice of Tiferet. In an arrogance consciousness, we assume we are superior. This allows us to exalt ourselves over the other, thus making the other feel small and unworthy.

Arrogance	The quality of character inclining one to be unduly or excessively superior, overbearing, exhibiting haughtiness, claiming more for itself and conceding little to others.

Once we have a mindset that we are superior, we have an unending desire to get what we want. We fall into the consciousness of lustfulness, the vice of Netzach. This is typically lustfulness for money, status, power, sex, or material things.

Lustfulness	The quality of character inclining one to such an intense eagerness and enthusiasm for the satisfaction of a desire, often a sexual desire, that the end becomes more important than the means.

With a lustfulness consciousness, what matters is the result and not how to get the result. So it is natural to fall into various kinds of unethical behavior centrally involving a consciousness of deceitfulness. This is the vice of Hod.

Deceitfulness	The quality of character which inclines one to have injurious intent while leading another person to believe something one knows is false.

To the extent that we have become successful in our deceitfulness, we work less and less. We become lazy. We fall into a slothfulness consciousness, the vice of Yesod.

Slothfulness	The quality of character which inclines one to be habitually lazy and move slowly when one knows that exertion or speed is essential.

Given a successful pattern of getting what we want, without much work, we become collectors of the things we have acquired, typically material things of value and/or money. Our consciousness has a strong component of avariciousness, the vice Malchut.

Avariciousness The quality of character inclining one to have an excessive and insatiable desire or passion for wealth, riches, or gain; cupidity, greediness.

Notice that in general terms when our consciousness is full of the vices of the tree of death, expansiveness is selfishly directed toward self. Contraction is directed toward the other. The beauty and balance that is suppose to happen in Tiferet, balances the expansiveness toward self with the contraction toward the other. The more the expansiveness toward self, the more the contraction toward the other. The victory and triumph that is suppose to happen in Netzach becomes a triumph because the obstacles we encounter diminish due to the energy and the passion of our lustfulness for the goal. The glory that is suppose to occur in Hod, becomes the glory of deceitful schemes, sometimes elaborately worked out deceitful schemes to get what we want at the expense of somebody else. The binding of our conscious determination to manifest the feelings of Chesed and Gevurah get reduced to a consciousness of laziness. Everything is being worked on nearly automatically. We need not toil. Our actions now just consist of collecting material things.

Tree of Death With Vices

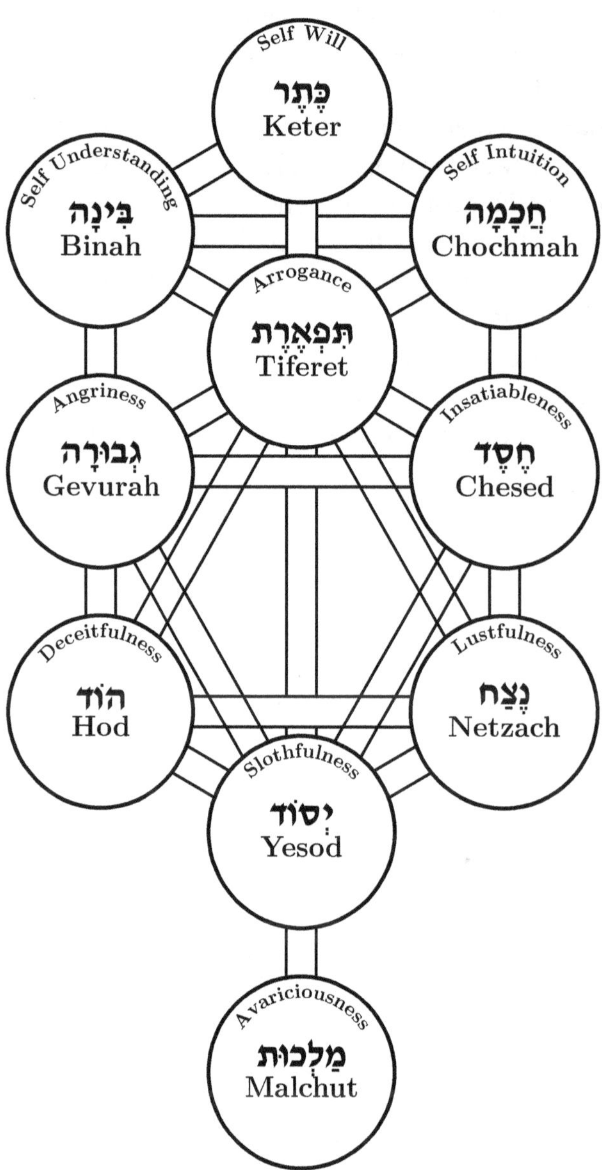

Figure 5: Shows the outermost vice structure of the Tree of Death.

The Tree of Life

Tree signifies nought but Torah for it is written:[1]

> *She is a Tree of Life to them that lay hold upon her.*
> *And happy is every one that holdeth her fast.*[2]
>
> *Her ways are ways of pleasantness,*
> *And all her paths are peace.*[3]

The Gerer Rabbi explained a parable in Midrash Rabbah.[4]

> A man fell from a boat into the sea; the skipper of the vessel threw him a rope and shouted:
>
> > Take hold of this rope, and do not let go; if you do, you will lose your life.
>
> The Rabbi then remarked:
>
> > This parable explains the verse
> >
> > > *She is a tree of life to them that lay hold upon her.*[5]
> >
> > If you let go of her, you will lose your life.[6]

Rabbi Jose of the Zohar teaches:

> How great is the power of the Torah, and how it is exalted above all, since he who occupies himself with the Torah fears no adversaries either above or below, nor any evil haps of the world, because he is attached to the Tree of Life and eats therefrom every day.[7]

Rabbi Judah of the Zohar teaches:

---

[1] *Midrash Rabbah*, Numbers 13:12, p. .524

[2] Proverbs .3:17

[3] Proverbs .3:18

[4] *Midrash Rabbah*, Numbers (17:7)

[5] Proverbs .3:18

[6] *The Hasidic Anthology*, Louis Newman, Schocken Books, New York, 1963, p.478.

[7] *The Zohar*, Vol V, Maurice Simon and Harry Sperling (translators), Soncino Press, London, 1978, p.341.

> The Tree of Life is the Torah, which is a great and mighty tree. It is called Torah (lit. showing) because it shows and reveals that which was hidden and unknown; and all life from above is comprised in it and issues from it. He that "takes hold" of the Torah takes hold of all, above and below.[8]

The Zohar ties the Tree of Life to the verse:

> *A river went forth from Eden.*[9]

The Zohar says:

> It has been laid down that the name of that river is Jubilee, but in the book of Rab Hammuna the Elder it is called Life, because life issues thence to the world. We have also laid down that the great and mighty Tree in which is food for all is called the Tree of Life, because its roots are in that Life. We have learned that the river sends forth deep streams with the oil of plenitude to water the Garden and feed the trees and shoots. These streams flow on and unite in two pillars which are called Yachin and Boaz.[10] Thence the streams flow on and come to rest in a grade called Zaddik, and from hence they flow further till they all are gathered into the place called Sea, which is the sea of Wisdom. But the current of that river never ceases, and therefore the streams flow back to the two pillars, Nezach and Hod, whence they traverse that Zaddik to find there blessings and joy. The Matrona is called the "time" of the Zaddik, and therefore all who are fed below are fed from this place, as it is written:
>
> > *The eyes of all wait on thee and thou givest them their meat in due season.*[11]
>
> When these two are joined, worlds have gladness and blessing, and there is peace among upper and lower beings. But when through the sins of this world there are not blessings from these streams, and the

---

[8] *The Zohar*, Vol V, Maurice Simon and Harry Sperling, Soncino Press, London, 1978, p.28.

[9] Genesis .2:10

[10] *And he set up the pillars in the porch of the temples;*
And he set up the right pillar, and called its name Yachin.
And he set up the left pillar, and called its name Boaz., 1 Kings .7:21 These are the left and right columns of the tree.

[11] Psalms .145:15

"time" sucks from the "other side," then judgement impends over the world and there is no peace.[12]

We read in the Zohar:

> There is a place on high that moves outwards and kindles all the lights on every side, and it is called *the world to come*, and from it a tree emerges in order to be nourished and prepared. This tree is exalted and honored above all the other trees. ... This world to come, which extends outwards cares for this tree all the time, watering it and preparing it through its work, crowning it with crowns, never at any time withholding its streams from it. Faith depends on this tree; it is more to be found in this tree than in any other tree; everything is sustained by it. For this reason it is written
>
> > *whatsoever God does it shall be forever*[13]
>
> – there is no doubt that He was, He is, and He will be –
>
> > *nothing can be added to it, nor anything taken from it.*[14]
>
> Therefore, it is written in the Torah,
>
> > *You shall not add to it, nor subtract from it*[15]
>
> for this tree is [the tree] of the Torah, and this place is cared for by God always.[16]

Again in the Zohar,

> He gave the Torah of truth, the Tree of Life, whoever takes hold of which achieves life in this world and in the world to come. Now the Tree of Life extends from above downward, and it is the Sun which illumines all. Its radiance commences at the top and extends through the whole trunk in a straight line. It is composed of two sides, one to the north, one to the south, one to the right and one to

---

[12] *The Zohar*, Vol V, Maurice Simon and Harry Sperling (translators), Soncino Press, London, 1978, p.38.

[13] Ecclesiastes .3:14

[14] Ecclesiastes .3:14

[15] Deuteronomy .13:1

[16] *The Zohar*, Vol. 3, Isaiah Tishby, David Goldstein (translator), Oxford University Press, London, 1991, pp.356-367.

the left. The "chamber" from which he goes forth is the starting-point of all. From that point he goes forth veritably as a bridegroom to meet his bride, the beloved of his soul, whom he receives with outstretched arm. The sun proceeds and makes his way toward the west; when the west is approached the north side bestirs itself to come forward to meet it, and joins it. Then

> *he rejoices as a strong man to run his course,*[17]

so as to shed his light on the moon. Now the words:

> *And the Lord spoke to Moses, saying, Speak to Aaron, and say to him, When thou lightest the lamps the seven lamps shall give light toward the body of the candlestick. And Aaron did so.*[18]

[These words] contain an allusion to the celestial lamps, all of which are lit up together from the radiance of the sun.[19]

Rabbi Hiya of the Zohar teaches the following interpretation of the verse:

> *For with thee is the fountain of life, in thy light we shall see light.*[20]

The fountain of life, he said, is the supernal oil which flows continually and is stored in the midst of that most high Wisdom, from which it never separates. It is the source which dispenses life to the supernal Tree and kindles the lights (of the emanations). And that tree is called the Tree of Life, because it is planted on account of that source of life. Therefore, too,

> *in thy light we shall see light*

in that light which is treasured for the righteous in the world to come and with which Israel will be illuminated.[21]

---

[17] Psalms .19:6

[18] Numbers .8:1-3

[19] *The Zohar*, Vol. V,Maurice Simon and Harry Sperling (translators), Soncino Press, London, 1978, p.203.

[20] Psalms .36:9

[21] *The Zohar*, Vol IV, Harry Sperling, Maurice Simon, and Paul Levertoff (translators), The Soncino Press, London, 1978, p.390.

Figure 6 shows the outer structure of the Tree of Life of Virtues. The virtue in Keter is will where will means a will aligned with God's will. This leads us to open the Hochmah channel to give us intuitions about bringing holiness in this world by our thoughts, speech, and action. And that which we understand by working out the details in Binah are all related to holiness.

The consciousness of lovingkindness, the virtue of Chesed, is felt not just with respect to ourselves but more importantly with respect to others.

Kindheartedness	The quality of character inclining one to have a good benevolent nature, consistently being helpful and showing consideration for others.

This consciousness of lovingkindness is reinforced with the consciousness of fortitude, the virtue of Gevurah: fortitude to keep the lovingkindness going and fortitude to limit it as appropriate.

Fortitude	The quality of character inclining one to have strength, moral endurance, patience and courage even under conditions of pain, privation, affliction, or temptation.

The consciousness of lovingkindness and fortitude are balanced just right in Tiferet where everything is wrapped in a consciousness of humility. Humility means we make room for others. We give them the opportunity to express themselves and we do not make any forcing moves or smothering moves. The consciousness of humility is the virtue of Tiferet.

Humility	The quality of character inclining one to be modest in feeling and manifesting one's own merits, self worth, or importance.

We pursue this consciousness of lovingkindness into action with the consciousness of dedicatedness, the virtue of Netzach.

Dedicatedness	The quality of character inclining one to be wholly committed to an ideal, a goal, a cause, a job, a family, or a project etc.

And we rationally work out the best mode of action by asking what if questions in Hod. The consciousness of rationality is the virtue of Hod.

Rationality	The quality of character inclining one to be agreeable to employ reason in developing an understanding of anything.

The consciousness of vigorousness is the virtue of Yesod. Vigorousness enables our lovingkindness to manifest in action.

Vigorousness	The quality of character inclining one to intense action which is full of energy and force.

The consciousness of industriousness is the virtue of Malchut. Not only are we able to bring out lovingkindness in proper measure but we are to be productive at the same time.

Industriousness	The quality of character inclining one to work energetically and devotedly.

Tree of Life With Virtues

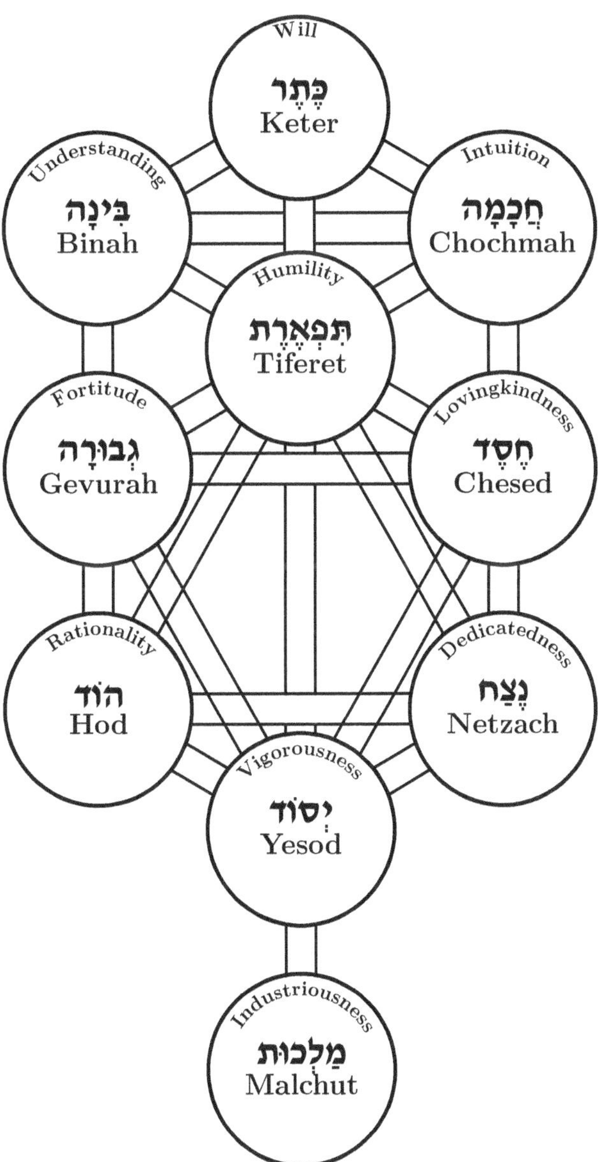

Figure 6: Shows the top level virtue structure of the Tree of Life.

Vice, Virtue, and Spirituality

In the last section we introduced the Tree of Death, with its top level vices and the Tree of Life with its top level virtues. In this section we will relate vices and virtues to spirituality.

A virtue is a character trait that guides a person to act, desire, and feel, involving the exercise of judgment and leads to a recognizable human excellence or instance of human flourishing.[1] For example, a virtuous person would act benevolently. But the benevolence is not to be benevolent or to be seen as benevolent, but because the appropriate response in the situation calls for benevolence. The virtue character trait can be summarized as a balanced excellence in thought, speech, and action.

Virtues are the character traits of a good person. The question of what is a good person is an old question. Plato defines being a good person as one with the character traits of wisdom, courage, self-restraint, and justice. Socrates defines being a good person as a person who lives virtuously and so becomes an ideal citizen. Aristotle defines a good person as one who is generous, friendly, truthful, and has greatness of soul. Aquinas listed the character traits of temperance, courageousness, justice, wisdom, faithfulness, hopefulness and charitableness.

The Book of Proverbs begins with an instruction for being a good person:

That men may know wisdom and instruction
Understand the words of insight,
Receive instruction in wise dealing,
Righteousness, justice, and equity,
That prudence may be given to the simple,
Knowledge and discretion to the youth,
The wise man also may hear and increase in learning,
And the man of understanding acquire skill
To understand a proverb and a figure,
The words of the wise and their riddles.[2]

Other verses in Proverbs advocate integrity, courage, righteousness, just leadership, trustworthiness, justice, love, graciousness, kindness, diligence, prudence, humility, temperance, hope, understanding, knowledge, respect for instruction, wisdom, and fear and love of God. In general the Torah defines a

[1] L.H. Yearley, *Mencius and Acquinas: Theories of virtues and conceptions of courage*, State University of New York Press, Albany, 1990, p. .13

[2] Proverbs 1:2-6

good person to be one who acts in accordance with the commandments given in the Torah.

Of course the list of virtues that we will encounter in the next sections includes all these. Our point is not just that virtuous behavior makes a good person and good citizen. It is not just that it is ethical and moral. It is that virtuous behavior helps us be God conscious, brings us closer to the Divine, and that being God conscious results in virtuous behavior. In short, spirituality manifested in behavior is virtuous behavior. Conversely, manifesting behavior that is vice separates us from God.

By cognitively studying the vices and the virtues and their definitions, it is possible to initiate a consciousness raising process and become more consciously sensitive. Let us consider one vice virtue contrast pair: arrogance and humility. Outwardly the arrogant person, is full of force, ready to put down others and take control. The force, however, is only self-serving. It exploits others for the selfish gain of the arrogant one. The force is divisive and therefore weakens. Humility appears to be weak. Spiritually, however, the person who is spiritually capable and powerful is the person with humility, for humility unifies and is life sustaining.

But there is more. When hard, challenging situations come to us, when we are in the dark, it is possible to transcend the darkness which is the appearance of the situation, and by appropriate understanding and virtuous behavior live through the difficulty by taking the opening that God gives us and bring Godliness into the world.

How can we get the wisdom to do this? By the right cognitive activity and the right communication and internal work with our emotional, subconscious, and soul levels. The cognitive activity is by understanding the structure of the vices on the tree of death and the virtues on the tree of life. The exercise prayer ritual activity is one way to do the internal work we do on ourselves to lessen our vices and increase our virtues. This internal work must connect and communicate to our emotional, subconscious, and soul levels. The structure of tree of death and the tree of life play the role of the spiritual organizing principles.[3]The exercise must be done with a full heart and intent. You will know that something has happened when you finish the exercise and you have a sense of an uplifting happiness and joy.

[3]The trees shown are the author's trees. Individual trees can differ from one another as they reflect the spiritual structure of the individual. You may use these trees as your initial guide. As you begin to understand their organizing principles, construct your own tree.

Chesed: *Giving or moving toward gone wrong*
Gevurah: *Moving away or inward gone wrong*
Tiferet: *Expanding or contracting gone wrong*
Netzach: *Moving toward without recognizing Divinity*
Hod: *Limiting by holding mind set static*
Yesod: *Connecting with purpose gone wrong*
Malchut: *Accumulating and preserving gone wrong*

Tree of Death With Vices

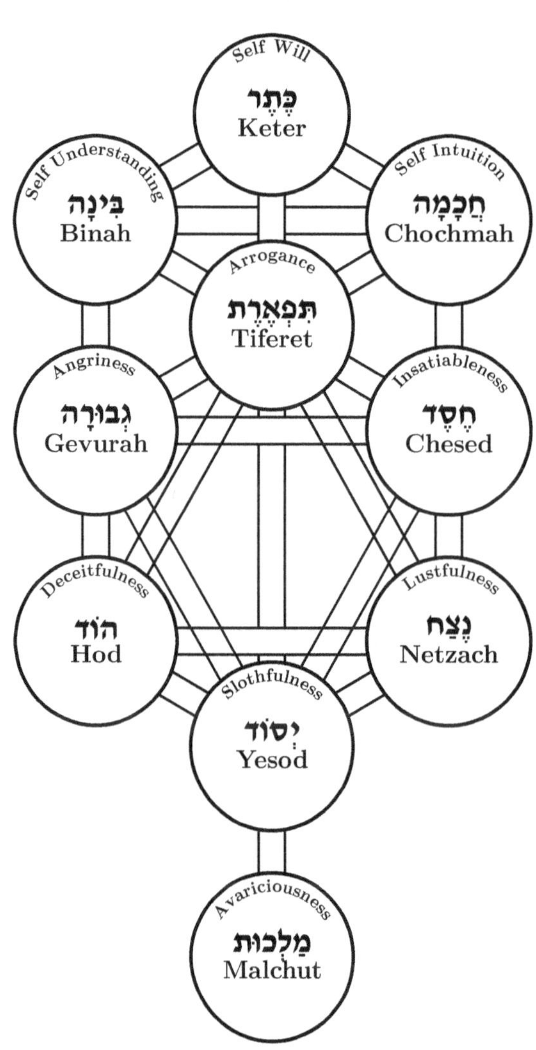

Preparation For Prayer

We must know that the words
Of our prayer have life.
By their life,
All Creation joins us in prayer.

We must know that the
Heaven and Earth were created
By the downward flow
Of the Divine letters.

We must know that
The life of our prayer
Arouses these letters
Through which all living things
Continue to be created.

Through uplifting the letters
We come to know
That our prayer is joined
To the Constant Flow of Creation:
Word to word, voice to voice,
Breath to Breath, thought to thought.

When our words fly upward
God turns toward the ascending word,
Then Life flows through all the worlds
And prayer receives its response.

We must know that
It is not the words themselves
That ascend to God.
It is the life of the words
That ascend.

The life of the words is:
The burning desire of our heart.
This is the essence of the words
That rises like smoke
Toward Heavenly reception.

We must put all of our strength
Into the words,
Proceeding from letter to letter,
With such concentration,
That we lose awareness
Of our bodily self.
So that it seems as if
The letters themselves
Are flowing into one another.

We must know that
Each word of prayer
Is a complete self.
If all of our strength is not in it,
It is born incomplete, deficient,
Lacking a limb.

We must focus all of our thoughts
On the Power of the words,
So that we may begin to see
The sparks of light
That shine within them.

We must know that the sacred letters
Are the chambers into which
God pours His flowing light.
The lights within each letter,
Ignite one another,
As they touch,
And new lights are born.

We must enter into the words,
Savoring their taste,
Speaking them with all our strength.
Then our soul,
Which is itself a part of God above.
Will meet God,
In the place of the word.

We must enter into the true union
With the Holy One of All Being.
We must enter into,
The Divine Presence:
With Hashem, יהוה , our God, אֱלֹהִים .

The Presence within us
Is *our God*, אֱלֹהִים ,
Joined together,
With Hashem, יהוה ,
Its eternal source.

We must make our prayer
Be pure and untainted,
So that the holy breath
That rises from our lips
Will join with the breath
Of Heaven that is always
Flowing into us from above.

We pray, to move ourselves closer to God,
To be more God conscious,
To become decent persons,
So that our giving will be a giving from our heart:
Our emotions will become all positive emotions,
And our actions will become all moral and ethical actions,
Actions that will bring virtue and Godliness in the world.

Every breath shall praise Him.
With each of our breaths,
We praise God.
As the breath leaves us,
It ascends to God,
And then it returns to us from above.
Thus that part of God,
That is within us,
Is reunited with its source.[1]

[1] About 20 years ago I was reading a book that had many of these lines which are in the spirit of the Baal Shem Tov teachings. I copied it down and then added to it. But when I went looking to locate the book so that I could acknowledge the source I was unable to find it.

Vice Virtue Prayer Ritual

The purpose of the vice virtue prayer ritual is to effect a change in our consciousness, making us more aware of whatever small part of us that brought into existence particular vices and to move away from this while moving toward that greater part of us that will bring even more virtue into existence. Or saying this another way, to move away from our evil inclination and toward our good inclination. So in this sense the ritual makes a break between what had been and what will be: a new beginning if you will.

The success of the vice virtue prayer ritual is dependent on your desire to change. Do this with all your heart. Focus your consciousness on the words and their meaning. Do not allow yourself to nurture any other thoughts besides the prayer ritual itself. Inflame yourself with the prayers.

The ritual begins with an invocation prayer, a prayer that blesses God and requests God's help in cleaving to the commandments, help in not being influenced by our evil inclination and help in being drawn toward our good inclination. This is a request to God to help us make the change in consciousness we desire. It has the form of a usual prayer. Many prayers might conclude at this point. But the vice virtue prayer ritual keeps going. This is just the opening part of the prayer ritual.

The second part of the prayer ritual is called voiding the other side. It is in a confession mode, but it does not have the part of asking forgiveness. Rather the perspective is that we have made mistakes, we take responsibility for those making those mistakes, and we take responsibility for changing in a way to lessen the possibility of making those mistakes again. Hence it is stronger than confession that asks for forgiveness. The emphasis is not on forgiveness. We admit the mistakes we have made and call out the specific vices we are working on, separating their past, our mistakes in manifesting them, from our future.

We make a promise to ourselves and God to voluntarily change our habitual consciousness and its conscious and subconscious desires and look at things from a different point of view, particularly the point of view of bringing virtue into existence. We put our consciousness in the mode that just as we are saying these words about the faults and mistakes we have made, the vices we have engaged in, we are changing. We banish from our consciousness, our hearts and minds, that which is unholy. We wipe out and void the class of vices we are working on, making them no longer be a part of ourselves. We void that part of us that is attached to the other side, the other side meaning that which is not holy.

After our voiding the other side we move into the third part, an even more active part of the vice virtue prayer ritual: the vows. We do something very intense and which is certainly not part of the usual prayer service. Using the first person plural, we make a vow, if you will a religious promise, to ourselves and to God, to manifest the holiness of God by the virtuous actions that we will do. And we call out the class of virtues toward which we wish to move.

The fourth part of the prayer ritual is transformation. There are two ways of transformation: by water or by fire. Typically this is done with water. For example the use of the Mikvah to purify ourselves. But the most powerful symbol for transformation, both physical and spiritual, is fire. Consider a couple of verses speaking about the era of moshiach.

> *And He shall sit as a refiner and purifier of silver; and he shall purify the sons of Levi, and purge them as gold and silver; and there shall be they that shall offer unto the LORD offerings in righteousness.*[1]

> *And I will bring the third part through the fire, and will refine them as silver is refined, and will try them as gold is tried; they shall call on My name, and I will answer them; I will say: 'It is My people', and they shall say: 'The LORD is my God.'*[2]

These verses put Hashem in the seat of the silversmith. In refining silver, the silversmith holds a piece of silver over the middle of the fire, where the flames are hottest and lets it heat up to burn away the impurities. In this way, fire becomes the metaphor for refinement of character traits.

Our ritual does not wait for the era of moshiach. We act in our time in our lives to refine ourselves. The ritual uses the imagery of fire in a third person mode of description. As we say the transformation part, we must visualize a wall of fire surrounding us, transforming and refining us, transforming the inner part of us. We engage ourselves in a guided visualization as we transcend from the person we were and move into the person we want to be.

The fifth part of the prayer ritual, its conclusion, in effect seals the transformation. Using the active first person voice in poetic rhyme, it describes that we are walking into the person we are to be. This is a person who identifies with his/her Godly soul. By acknowledging that identity we bind ourselves to the Divine, moving ourselves closer to Hashem. Spiritually, we become Divine in nature bound. We acknowledge that which is transcendent by the symbology of heaven, the stars, the dark deep space and bring them to us as they shine in our embrace.

---

[1] Malachi 3:3

[2] Zacheriah 13:9

The symbolism here is certainly not one of worshipping the sky or stars or deep space. Recall the beginning verses of Psalms 148.

> Halleluyah! Praise God from the heavens.
> Praise Him in the heights.
> Praise Him, all His angels,
> Praise Him all His Legions.
> Praise Him, sun and moon;
> Praise Him all the bright stars.
> Praise Him the most exalted of the heavens
> And waters that are above the heavens.

All that which is beyond us praises God so we also should praise God. In the metaphor of our prayer, we embrace and become part of all of that which is praising God. We embrace heaven. We embrace the stars. We embrace the dark deep space – the heights of Psalm 148. And they all shine in our embrace, meaning that they all are praising God with us. But our praise of God is not the Halleluyah praise of Psalm 148. It is a deeper and stronger praise. We praise God by transcending the person we were and moving toward the person we want to be, a new person closer to God. That is the strongest praise possible – to relate with virtue to our reality and the people in our reality as God would want us to relate to our reality and indeed as we imagine how God Himself relates with His virtue to the reality he created.

The symbol of the transformed person is the burning candle within for it gives light, a light that unifies the left and the right. The left and the right are the left and right columns of the tree of life. Unifies means balancing them so we manifest the right amount of expansion and the right amount of contraction. It also means unifying the appearance and the essence, a topic we extensively explored. The symbology of the unification is the wedding. If you will, appearance and essence wed.

The concluding verses of the prayer ritual is a blessing. We have come to a more spiritually elevated state. We bless everything that is happening to us: we bless the coming; we bless the going. We bless the call from God to move toward that which is holy. We bless God, by blessing the One and then by blessing it All. The One of course is God. The All is the manyfoldness of our reality for all of the manyfoldness is connected to God, indeed has a Divine connection to God. And all this is also One. So by saying the concluding verses, we make a unification. Any such unification is a praise and blessing to God.

The vice and virtues in the following prayer ritual are those of the top level structure of the tree as shown in figures 5 and 6. The second volume *God Consciousness: Working the Sefirot and Netivot* will go deeper into the vice virtue structure of each of the lower seven Sefirot for there is a tree within each of the lower seven Sefirot. On the lower seven Sefirot of these inner trees is a refined set of vices and virtues that give the structure to the vices and virtue of the Sefirot containing them.

Invocation

Divine,
Eternal,
Holy One of All Being,
Thou who art God of the Universe,
Thou who art Father of Abraham, Isaac, and Jacob,
We bless Thee.

We call to Thee,
Who formest light and givest us understanding,
Who createst darkness and givest us wisdom,
Whose miracles are with us daily,
And whose glory and honor fill all the earth.

Help us to cleave to thy commandments,
So that we will not be influenced by our Evil Inclination.
So that we will be drawn to our Good Inclination.
And we will be kept away from vice.
And drawn toward virtue.

Return us, our God, to Thy Torah,
Draw us closer to Thy service,
Help us become perfect before Thee,
We bless Thee, who desires our return,
Our Teshuvah, תְּשׁוּבָה.

Voiding The Other Side

Divine,
Holy,
Eternal One of All Being,
All knowing one,
Come forward and listen to our souls.
We have manifested human frailties.

Because of the faults we have committed,
And because of the faults we have attempted to commit
By intention, thought, speech, or action,
We are changing.

Banished from our minds are,
Unholy desires and thoughts.
Banished from our hearts are:

Insatiableness,
Angriness,
Arrogance,
Lustfulness,
Deceitfulness,
Slothfulness,
Avariciousness.

Void is the other side.

Our Vows

All knowing One come forward and listen to our hearts.
From this moment we renew our vows to bring earth to heaven,
To bring help and light to those in darkness,
To give courage and hope to the needy,
To scatter the dense mass of delusion and misery,
To nurture all things worthwhile and virtuous.

We vow to be compassionate, gentle, and humble,
To manifest truth, beauty, joy, and love in all we do.
We vow to be a symbol of the pure,
We vow to manifest your presence by acting with:

Lovingkindness,
Fortitude,
Humility,
Devotedness,
Rationality,
Vigorousness,
Industriousness.

All knowing One come forward and listen to our heart.
We will manifest your presence by our actions.

Transforming

Around us is a wall of fire.
Fire transforms the inner.
Appearance ascends.
Essence descends.

The connection is activated.
We are transcending out of the persons we were,
And into the persons we are to be.
Glowing with light are our:

> Lovingkindness,
> Fortitude,
> Humility,
> Devotedness,
> Rationality,
> Vigorousness,
> Industriousness.

Being Transformed

I am walking into the person I am to be,
The humble, gentle, and kind soul that is me,
My own true self I am to found,
Divine in nature bound.

The Heaven above enclothes me.
The circle of stars does plea
That the sea of dark deep space
Shines in my embrace.

Within me burns the candle of light
Uniting the left and the right.
Appearance and essence in bed
On level upon level wed.

I bless the coming,
I bless the going,
I bless the call,
I bless the One,
I bless it ALL.

The Torah of Moshiach

When things happen that are challenging:
Somebody else makes a mistake or we make a mistake,
Think of it as a missed play.

A missed play does not make the world imperfect.
God's world in all its perceived imperfections is perfect.

When a missed play occurs
It becomes the opportunity that God gives us
To bring virtue into the world.
If you will, God is hiding and is asking us,

> Can you nevertheless find me?
> Can you see me?
> Can you be close to me, even now?

The Zohar tells us that when we come
To the Divine Court of Truth,
The first question we are going to be asked is:
What evil did you turn to good?

When we act in a way
That takes what has the appearance of bad
And turn it into good,
We bring virtue into the world.
That is what the Torah of Moshiach guides us to do.

But why does God hide?
Virtue cannot be brought into manifestation
If the world had the appearance of perfection.
But a perfect world can have an appearance of imperfection.
By our actions, we can change our consciousness:
The imperfect appearances can be changed
Into perfect appearances.

This is how the Torah of Moshiach tells us to bless God:
By acting in a way that our consciousness changes
What has the appearance of imperfection
Into the appearance of perfection.

Thereby, we bless God.

For God does not hide.
It is our own consciousness that hides God from us.

The Torah of Moshiach

Index

www.ingramcontent.com/pod-product-compliance
Lightning Source LLC
Chambersburg PA
CBHW080514090426
42734CB00015B/3048